Trusting Your Intuition

Discover Your Superpower in 10 Days

JACQUELINE BEST

Contact: Jacqueline Best at **bestwholenewworld@gmail.com**

Published by: Jacqueline Best

First Edition, 2020

Additional Contact Information:

https://www.youtube.com/jacquelinebest

https://www.facebook.com/bestwholenewworld/

https://www.instagram.com/bestwholenewworld/

https://twitter.com/bestwholenew

TABLE OF CONTENTS

THE GIFT OF SHADOW

This book is dedicated to Shadow, who taught me to overcome my fear of the unknown, and trust the process.

My daughters' had desired a dog from a very early age. I would respond, "In the right time." I was hoping that "the right time" would be when they had grown up and moved out of the house.

After Christmas 2008, we walked into a health food store, to meet the owner that was helping support our home school's water fundraiser for Ecuador.

As soon as we walked through the door, he said, "You look like a family that needs a dog." Before we could even respond, he had picked up the phone, and made a call. There was no answer, so he left a message saying he may have a family for the dog. My daughters were excited and I was observing the process as he seemed to be taking charge. He explained that a woman had just left his store, saying that she needed to help her brother out, and find a home for a Labrador puppy.

As we were about to leave the store, the phone rang, and it was the woman. I spoke with her briefly. She had explained that her brother was recently divorced, and had bought a purebred black lab for his 15 years old son to ease the pain. Between work, school and hockey games, the dog was getting no attention, and he realized this wasn't a good idea.

By that evening, we had met four month old Shadow. I knew this was "the right time". On January 1st, our black velveteen rabbit named "Lucky" went out the front door to his new family, and Shadow walked in the back door to be with us. It was like our pet had grown in an instant!

During the two week trial, Shadow bit my former husband, had many wild ways of running around in a circle, chasing his tail, and was very dominant. Many friends and family expressed their reservations about the extra cost of a dog. It was irrelevant to me. I trusted the process.

I knew, "this was the right time." A wild black dog named Shadow. How could the Universe be any more clear. It was time to overcome my fears and embrace my own shadow!

Once the two week trial was over, the owner passed over the pure bred ownership certificate and gave us $500 to take care of him. I was stunned. Very few people are given a 4 month old pure bred lab plus an extra $500 to take care of him.

Shadow was a gift in many ways. I could have easily said, "No" for logical reasons. He taught me to be open to receive and to live more in the moment. As you read the book, you will see from my experiences that Carl Jung's quote is true.

"The most intense conflicts, if overcome, leave behind a sense of security and calm that is not easily disturbed."

Shadow was the gift that loved me through the process of transformation, breakdown to breakthrough. I became aware to totally trust my inner guidance, and that Source / consciousness is always granting my heart's desires in wonderful ways!

Each Experience is a Gift, as it is the Present

*It's the meaning that we give the experience
that creates different results.*

I never questioned the ways of the world, until my mid 20's. I did all the so-called "right" things like get a University degree, get a good career, and make lots of money. I was taught money would give me choices.

Financial resources and material possessions were always abundant, relationships had issues, and health problems were considered normal.

At a young 28 years, back in 1991, my life of business travel, planes, hotels and meeting clients for lunch/dinner lost its glamour. The company car, expense account, my condo, private golf membership and all my designer clothes etc., could not ease this feeling inside me that "this can't be the point of life?"

I wanted off the treadmill, out of the rat race, and to find my truth. I wanted a peace within myself and the freedom to live my life on my terms. The truth was, that I didn't know what I wanted, except to stop feeling stressed and miserable on the inside. I had never thought about what I wanted; as in what gives me joy. I only thought about what I was to do that would give me lots of money, so I would have freedom. In the world I grew up in, money provided choices.

What I discovered is that money can help with your health, but it can't guarantee you health and well being in body, mind, and spirit. This is what I wanted. This was my heart's desire. To have the awe of a child. To be truly free!

I never knew this was the journey I was on, to heal from the inside out, and then help others trust their intuition/inner guidance to do the same.

From Louise Hay, Deepak Chopra, to Ekhart Tolle, Abraham, Wayne Dyer, and a vast array of other authors, I took a deep dive into all things alternative. I read countless books and went to many spiritual and personal development events.

Everything I was exposed to had an impact on me. There was relief in many areas of my life, but I still felt like I was searching for the Holy Grail. All were pieces of the puzzle, but none of them felt like they gave me all the answers I was seeking.

After a *You Can Heal Your Life* event, I was given CD's of all the speakers, because I was a volunteer. I heard Dr. Christiane Northrup mention this man Bruno Groening. When I googled I discovered there were healings of biblical nature attributed to him that had occurred in Germany after WWII.

I was surprised because I had never heard of him. My daughters were at the Toronto Waldorf School which was inspired by Rudolph Steiner from Germany. Most of the families were very alternative and spiritual. Yet he was unknown to all of us.

When I read the words of Bruno Groning, **"You don't have to believe a word I say, but you have a duty to convince yourself,"** I thought how freeing. I get to decide!

It has nothing to do with someone else's opinions or experiences. It is solely my job to convince myself of what is true.

I put every idea aside, and every book back on the book shelf. I decided I would have my experience, and let my experience be my proof.

What I discovered was life altering. Completely transformative. I'll use my experiences with meditation and prayer as examples.

When **I prayed**, I was asking God for help or being grateful or setting intentions. I was talking to God.

When **I meditated**, I was connecting with this all expansive Universe that filled my soul, but it took a lot of mindfulness to be present. I noticed I was more than my thoughts.

When **I tuned into the healing streams** that Bruno said were present, I simply received the whole power of the Universe coming into my body. Oneness.

I also have that similar experience when I gaze with Braco. I realize I'm the character, the vessel, and Source / consciousness provides the script, the flow, that comes through my inner guidance.

The suffering I experienced in my life led me to have a deep desire for relief. The answers came through my inner guidance. It was up to me to have the courage to follow. I could never have imagined my journey. Inner guidance took me and will take you, to experiences you never, ever thought about. It will take you to places or people better than you imagined. It will also release you from the bondage, the hurt, and the pain.

This book comes from the Source / consciousness. It provides you an outline so you too can have your unique experiences, without you delving into Bruno's teaching, joining the Circle of Friends, or gazing with Braco. I encourage you to have your own experience over these 10 days. Let your experiences be your teacher. I will be the guide.

This is about you transforming from the Caterpillar world to the Butterfly world. From struggling, doubting, suffering, to freedom, health, and confidence that Joy, Health, Peace, Love and Wealth exist all the time. You may be entering the chrysalis of transformation, have been there for a while, or about to burst out and fly. Relax and trust the process. You'll be introduced to a whole new world. Your Best Whole New World. This is the beginning to Surrender - the Ultimate Trust!

My Journey to Surrender - the Ultimate Trust

The world is easing lockdown, as I finish this book. My Superpower was tuned in well ahead of the news. I was guided on Feb 3rd to book a flight to return home from Costa Rica eight days before the virus was even named by the World Health Organization (WHO). My Canadian and American friends questioned my guidance, as their logic said, it's "cold up north!" None of us had heard anything until Feb 28th.

I had an enjoyable flight home and was safely back in Toronto, Canada on March 3th. Nine days later WHO announced the global pandemic. The others scrambled with stress and anxiety to find a flight near the end of March. I did 21 days in Toronto before I was guided home to Prince Edward Island, where there has been a 100% recovery rate with no hospitalizations. I'm grateful that my Superpower always knows what's best for me! I live in the Butterfly World which is a different world than the Caterpillar World. Butterflies always trust their Superpower to lead the way! It's full of Joy, Health, Peace, Love and Wealth!

Welcome to Trusting your Intuition - Discover your Superpower in 10 days!

I am happy to be your guide on this 10 day experience as you journey from caterpillar to butterfly. It will take you from relying on outside sources for your decisions, to developing your Superpower, so you can trust your own inner guidance.

Here's a little bit of background, and part of my journey in learning to trust my inner guidance. These events were the start of me having confidence that everyone's inner guidance can lead them to their best whole new world. Now I live in Surrender, and I am an open channel for the script/the guidance that comes through me.

My first big jump into the unknown world of trusting my intuition/inner guidance was back in 1991, when I left my successful career at the age of 28 and took off to Africa. This was a key moment in my life. I learned what I felt within myself was more important than others' opinions of my actions or their beliefs.

After spending four months travelling in Eastern and Southern Africa, I had learned many things about myself. I knew that I could never go back to Canada and participate in the so-called real world again the same way. The concept of trading happiness for money no longer made sense to me.

I was completely in the dark about what I was going to do if I didn't go back to corporate, and had to trust the process. Over the decades, I went from trusting on some things to still doubting in other areas. I managed to stay self employed, and raise my daughters completely opposite to my upbringing, as I honed my trust and belief in my Superpower.

The summer of 2014 was a critical time in following my inner guidance. It was a whole new level of trust. It was my "Master's exam". From that experience I have learned to live in Surrender - the Ultimate Trust.

I was guided to purge a nearly 3000 square foot house. It needed to be completed in 30 days. I was guided to let it all go. I was giving away things for $20 if you could carry it, and $40 if it took two people to carry it, even the piano! There was so much stuff. You know how it is in a house. It seems that closets, cupboards and drawers are endless.

I had a friend bring women from the Salvation Army to take whatever they could use, as there were so many household items. A minister came by to pick up a couple of the ladies, and she questioned me about giving away necessity items that I would need again wherever I relocated. I informed her that I was directed by God to give them all away, and I trusted the process.

My two daughters and our beloved dog, Shadow, got into our car, having let go of our home. I was calling it a summer adventure that would lead us to our new home. We wanted to go West or maybe to Northern Ontario. Yet, we were guided every step of the way to go East. We tuned in, and followed the answers we received.

We would only make decisions when all of us would get the same answer. About 95% of the time, we were always in agreement. Occasionally, there was one of us that received a different answer, so we'd do it again. My rationale was if it was in all of our highest and best good, the answers would be the same. Essentially every time we got to a fork in the road, we tuned in to our inner guidance.

We were led to Prince Edward Island (PEI). We had to cross a 12 kilometer bridge to get to the Island. There was even a beautiful sunrise to greet us. It was like crossing over into a whole new world.

When we arrived I was thinking, "We have other provinces to go and see." I was thinking, "We're going to make this a great road trip, and eventually get out West." I was attached to the idea of a cross Canada road trip. That wasn't the plan. Things started to fall into alignment very quickly.

My youngest had been homeschooled, or more appropriately unschooled, and there were zero plans to go to high school. One day, I was walking the dog in an area where we had parked the car. I discovered the local high school. I felt like, " Wow! This school is calling to Faith." I came back and suggested that she go take a walk and check it out. She walked around the school. She felt the same thing. The school was saying, "It's time for you to come."

This occurred 13 days before school was to begin in September. When we walked into the school the next day, to find out about admissions, the only person there was the vocal teacher. This was perfect. Faith loved to sing and has had lyrics flow out of her constantly since childhood. She found out there was a great musical program, with a planned trip to perform at Disney World too!

The next day my eldest daughter saw a college. She was curious. She went in and discovered that they had a contemporary music program. She was classically trained in opera, so it didn't seem to make sense, but yet she felt like making the inquiry. They asked her to come audition two days later.

Within eleven days she was walking into her first day of college. We went with the process. We never asked about the cost, or considered that she was unschooled since grade three. Everything came together perfectly. She was admitted without transcripts and tuition was paid in full on the last day before it was due.

We looked around for a place to live, but nothing felt 100% right. There was a house that I wanted to have work as it seemed to have everything we needed. It felt good, like an 8 or 9 out of 10. I wanted to say it was good enough because it would make us feel better that we had a place to live. But when we tuned in, the answer was, "No."

We returned to Toronto to say goodbyes, pick up the few items we had left behind, and head back to PEI. We arrived without having a place to live in, and everyone questioned our choice as the rental market had almost no vacancies.

We trusted and were patient. Three days passed, until the right place came onto the market. We saw it three days later. The pictures all looked good, but when we finally saw it, it was more than perfect.

We were guided to live on 55 acres with a man-made pond that I was able to swim in. The owners, themselves, had built this 50 metre pond, and had only used it once. It was like my own private swimming pool, and as a swimmer, it was pure joy. There were private walking trails through the forest and farm, that led right to the town's soccer fields. There was freedom for Shadow to run, and plus he had another dog to play with now. Being a lab, having a dog, a pond, and a place to run, he was in dog heaven.

Everything was furnished here, to the tiniest detail. Source /consciousness knew what was ahead of me and why it made sense to let everything go. We each had a queen size bed. Parking in a heated garage. A sauna in our bathroom. It truly was perfectly designed for our needs. It was a ten minute bicycle ride for Faith to go to high school, and located perfectly between access to the town, the beach, and serenity of the countryside.

The landlord was such a blessing as she took care of everything. She tended the organic garden, and made sure that I had enough organic food to eat. She took care of the pond, so I could swim and enjoy it. I took the dogs for strolls on the walking trails, while she cut the grass on all that acreage.

PEI had the most snow in it's history that winter. Over 250 cm.

(over 8 ft)! She made sure that the walkways and the driveway were plowed for me to go to work. It was a huge blessing. Everything was taken care of for us.

I was very glad I listened to my inner guidance, and never got the other house where I would have had to DO everything. Even my agnostic, perfectionist father said, "It's amazing. Everything has seemed to work out perfectly for all of you."

My story continues from there, with one guided step after another, always being led to my heart's desires. I move with ease and grace, always one step ahead of oncoming storms. I trust my inner guidance, while others rely on outside sources leading them to experience stress, confusion, and anxiety.

I am encouraging you to have your own experiences. My experience might inspire you, but it is through your experiences that you will convince yourself. You will learn to discern and become more aware of the experiences in your body, mind and spirit.

This 10 day experience is about you learning to have complete confidence at every turn in the road. As you tune in, you will find out which way is best for you. That's what really matters, that you find your way on this journey, and are confident of your choices as you transform from caterpillar to butterfly.

I believe that every person's inner guidance is programmed to show them the way to their heart's desires. Those desires are there for you to take action on and follow in this life. Experiencing how those heart's desires occur is the essence of LIFE. It's time to enjoy all of your life, isn't it?

Let your heart's desires bubble up, and we will take the first step to

Trusting your Intuition - Discover your Superpower in 10 days.

As I've surrendered, I realize I am an open channel for the Vision that comes through me.

"One billion people being healed from the inside out, trusting their inner guidance, enjoying the journey to their heart's desires, and living in their best whole new world."

Are you ready to leave the Caterpillar World behind, and enter the Chrysalis of transformation? Let's get started!

WHAT OTHERS ARE SAYING

Annelle from Poland:

I had my aha moment on day 3. Your question, 'What is the pay off for me to keep listening?' was just perfect!

I realized that one of my patterns in listening was that I'm confused and don't know what steps to take. It was a pattern that was showing up often with my work and was always slowing me back and making me feel stuck.

I watched your day 3 video and your question popped out which gave me a final aha moment, that I don't have to listen to the parts of me that tell me I'm confused anymore.

Our guidance speaks to us all the time. Thank you very much beautiful Jacqueline.

Barbara from USA:

Thank You for this journey of self-awareness that ISSSS blooming everyday. Opening up to the wonders of the Universe to see & experience. My body was overloaded yesterday, so I took a day off, rested, ANNND I'm back on the right track today.

I'll make sure that everyday I'll do what brings me JOY, HAPPINESS, BLISS, etc, anything my heart desires!!!!! I'll keep tuned into the right channel & shoot for the stars!!!!

Sujata from Australia

Thanks for the inspiring video Jacqueline. Listening to the body is something I often overlook and forget even though I know I should!! Yet another reminder to be mindful. I know my body is at ease when I am surrounded by the beauty of nature for sure. And of course the noticeable resistance in the body when I have to do something that I really don't want to do.

Shelly from USA:

Thank you! Had a big AHA this weekend! I 100% believe in magic/flow/the mystery. Upon receiving the magic, experiencing the mystery face to face I almost immediately Make It Mean Something - as in try to organize it, understand it, figure a plan from it. Doing this creates stress in me as I create a list of things I need to do with this opportunity, person or inspiration. It can often create disappointment and doubt as well when it didn't turn out how I expected. WOW! This is so profound for me! I feel an opening to freedom - an invitation to be free to be, listen, enjoy and receive. Free to enjoy the spaciousness of not working so hard to Figure and Do and Get Somewhere. Yippee and thank you! Your messages are so rich and clear. Just amazing! xoxoxo.

Razia from South Africa

Jacqueline, I've been tuning in all weekend even if I got the words wrong ☐ I've been calm and trusted that everything would be done for my best and highest good 🙈 I'm back home now.

Carol from the USA:

This has been the most challenging part of the journey so far, letting everything I thought I knew go.... Each day I start with a clean slate, new beginning and let it all go. I am aware of feeling lighter and happier than I have for a long time. Doing all the "work" to release, refine, identify, learn, etc and not achieving the peace I thought would occur over the years has been disheartening. Letting all the things I thought I knew go has actually been freeing, instead of scary. This 10 day journey has been a blessing in my life. Looking forward to each new day.

Shweta from Netherlands

Listening to my inner voice & my dream 🏯 It is helping me big time & people around me 👪... feel blessed that I am able to reach out to people & help them in some way & further heal myself & feel peace within. Thank you Jacqueline.

Ragna from Norway

I had a session with Jaqueline on Sunday, and I highly recommend you to have one too if you have some limiting beliefs that's stopping you moving forward. We found a very important belief right away that really made me understand a few things on a deeper level, and it needed to go for me to be myself and take place in my body.

It felt so good after, especially because it was amazing to throw the paper with the old beliefs and let them go. Since then I've been releasing emotions that've been stuck in my body.. and it continues. I was a lot more present, feeling, listening. I realised that I don't have to be happy all the time, I am human and all emotions are part of life 💜<3How boring would life be without them! Coming back 😊:-*

Elena from Italy:

Day 5: Your video has been powerful for me today. Your words about stress are opening a "dialogue" about how my inner guidance spoke and speaks...while I seldom listened to her. Today is different and I've listened (saying no to a false opportunity). It's working!

How to use this Book for your Best Results

I recommend you read a chapter each day.

Follow along sequentially.

Do the Energetic Tune-In daily, and write the answers to the questions in each chapter.

Be aware of your experiences during each day, and note or share with others.

The Energetic Tune-In:

This is key. I've put it at the beginning and end of each chapter, to remind you to do it. It's that important. It only takes a few minutes and it will change your life.

I've found that it's best for me to have my feet flat on the floor, legs slightly apart, palms up ready to receive a gift.

I do it sitting or standing, eyes open or closed, and always get present to a joyful feeling and thought.

If you have a difficulty finding a joyful feeling and thought, look outside at nature or play a piece of music that will help open you to gratitude and a better feeling.

In the beginning, I never felt anything in my body. I just opened and received, and then one day I noticed I was feeling happier. Then I started to feel tingles, and it progressed from there.

As always, you can benefit from doing the Tune-In with me.

https://youtu.be/LNazErJFVgs

Can you do it other ways?

Yes, you can. I've done it different ways. I've convinced myself that I receive the most powerful charge sitting or standing in an open posture.

Journal:

Get a notebook or use Notes on your phone, for the 10 day experience, to record your thoughts on this journey. You will use it daily to answer questions, to write down experiences that you received an "aha," and other thoughts.

Facebook Group:

Within the Facebook group I have recorded many Facebook live videos. Each video is labeled #live #day1, #day2, etc., for you to easily search and watch if you need more of my experience. Each #live has a tune-in at the end, and most people find tuning in with me has more energy than just doing it on your own. You will find many Tune-Ins in the Facebook group, just search #live #tunein.

I've done my best to share many different experiences, in a variety of ways, in order to help you on your journey. In addition, I have answered some questions and go further in depth on some of the Facebook lives, as everyone is at a different place in trusting their inner guidance.

There are many video testimonials included in the book. Each person shares how these 10 days have changed their lives and their connection to their Superpower. Their inner guidance has strengthened each time they repeated the 10 day experience.

If you want to connect with the Facebook group, here are a couple options to introduce yourself:

- Trust the process and hit the Facebook Live button. Say your name, where you are from, what you believe about your inner guidance and what you hope to gain from the experience.
- Post a selfie with the number you rated yourself regarding how well you are following your inner guidance.
- Post a photo of you in a place that gives you a deep sense of connecting to your inner guidance and let us know why you are doing the 10 days, and how you hope to benefit externally and internally.

You can participate in different ways:

- Encouraging others to keep moving forward.
- Acknowledging that you felt the same.
- Noticing similarities or differences in each experience.

Each inner guidance system works differently and always delivers great results!

Facebook group:

https://www.facebook.com/groups/1966094080331136/

Day 1 - Trusting Your Intuition Discover Your Superpower in 10 days

I am going to be your guide during this 10 day experience. This time will be special and unique just for you, because the insights will be yours alone.

Get a notebook or use Notes on your phone to record your thoughts on this journey. You will use it daily to answer questions, to write down experiences where you received an "aha," and other thoughts.

Follow along, one day at a time, doing the Tune-In and contemplating the topic for the day. I know you will become more confident in Trusting Your Intuition/Inner Guidance, and realize the Superpower within you if you do the Tune-In daily.

It is important to participate each day.

Your experience will be unique to you and entirely different from anyone else's. It will allow you to convince yourself of how your inner guidance communicates with you. Along this journey, you will discover that Source / consciousness is actually always granting your heart's desires in wonderful ways that you never imagined.

You will become confident in your guidance even when others are questioning you or the world outside yourself seems to be going in a different direction.

It's going to take about 10 to 15 minutes of your day to get the benefits

You are going to engage with yourself, have your own personal experiences, and learn to recognize your own Superpower that is inside you.

This is about looking inside, instead of outside, for validity on your path. Appearances can be deceptive, but your inner guidance is always perfect for you.

Again it's up to you to have your own experience and convince yourself of your Superpower.

Convincing Yourself

I want you to take everything you know and set it aside. This includes your beliefs whether you are a spiritualist, a scientist, or deeply religious.

Take everything that you know, what you think you know about science, religion, and the universe, and put it aside for 10 days, OK?

You can always go back to everything you "know" after the ten days are finished.

I'm encouraging you to allow your experience here to convince you of the truth of your inner guidance. Your "knowing" can get in the way.

Consider that the Universe is like a big circle:

One part is you know, what you know - you know your name

One part is you know, what you don't know - you know you can't walk on water

One part is you don't know, what you don't know - the biggest part of the circle

During this 10 day experience, your inner guidance is going to take you into the biggest part of the circle, **"you don't know, what you don't know."**

In the same way, the higher up the mountain you go, your view becomes more expansive, and you see things entirely differently. You get to experience a whole new world. Does everyone at the bottom of the mountain, or half way up, experience the view like at the top of the mountain?

Are you open to putting what you think you "know" to the side for the full effects of this experience?

If you are saying, "yes," get ready, as I'm going to take you from your mind to your heart. To reach your Best Whole New World, we will travel from the Caterpillar World, through the Chrysalis of Transformation to the Butterfly World.

If you have beliefs that you have to be mindful, or change your mindset, or clear your subconscious to be in the flow, then give up those beliefs for the next 10 days too.

Science is proving that the heart sends more messages to your brain than your brain sends to the heart, and that your heart is also in coherence with the magnetism of the whole earth. Heart-centredness has a whole new meaning if it's connected to the planet, right?

I am going to focus on the heart as the pulse of your inner guidance

With each beat of your heart, you are being reminded of your connection to Source / consciousness. Notice how you feel when you focus on this heart connection instead of your breath. It is symbolic of the LOVE that guides for your highest and best good.

Are you willing to check everything you know and put it aside for 10 days to convince yourself of your Superpower?

If you are resisting, remind yourself of why you were led to this book.

Step 2: Grab your notebook or open Notes, and answer the questions

If you have any thoughts bothering you about what I am saying, take a moment and write out these thoughts in your notebook. This will help you with your experience.

I'm also going to share my experiences as we go along.

You will read how my free will only chooses to follow my inner guidance consistently. I have convinced myself that my inner guidance always leads me to my heart's desires, and it's better than I ever imagined.

I call it Surrender - the Ultimate Trust. It's living only from my inner guidance. Nothing else matters. It's living in the NOW. It's a "being" state versus a "thinking" state. It's natural once you reset, reactivate, and reconnect to your Superpower.

I completely trust the process of life moment by moment. All there ever is, is NOW, the gift of the present.

I'm here to help you discover what's true for you, so you can use your own Superpower to guide you for your highest and best good.

Write in your notebook, "I'm setting aside everything I think I know for the 10 day experience. I can pick up those beliefs again on the 11th day if I choose."

Is there a "but" or an "except" there for you, write out your reason or rationale behind your excuses.

What do you Believe about your Inner Guidance?

It doesn't matter what I believe or what anybody else believes about their inner guidance. It only matters what you believe. Your belief is creating the foundation for your own inner guidance experiences in your own life.

The goal of this book is for you to learn what your intuition/inner guidance feels like for you. How it communicates with you. What happens when you resist, or when you follow what you believe to be your inner guidance.

Write, **"I believe .... about my inner guidance system." (fill in the gap)**

This could be a sentence or a paragraph. It's your belief. Write the thoughts that come to you. All of them.

On a scale of 1 to 10, using 1 as "not at all" and 10 as "every moment" rate the following statement:

How well are you following your inner guidance today? Rate it 1-10

Now, consider the following question and provide enough information to clearly connect with those thoughts and emotions which keep you from following your inner guidance.

What is stopping you from always following your inner guidance?

Again, this could be a sentence like, "I'm not sure," or there could be a whole story that you need to let out so you can actually get present to the thoughts that affect you.

Now, did you open up your notebook or Notes and answer those three questions?

I highly recommend that you do. It's beneficial for you to write the answers down before moving on.

Early Memory of Inner Guidance

I want you to remember a time, an early memory, when you were feeling something different than what you were being told.

My experience

I always had a snapshot in my mind of my grandad and I playing 'tea time' with my tiny table and chairs, when I was three years of age. When I actually allowed myself to remember, he had buckled over grabbing his stomach. He told me he was fine and not to tell my mom what happened. It was our secret. I knew he was in pain. I felt like I had to tell my mom, but I went along with him.

Three months later, my grandad died.

As a three year old, I thought I was to blame for his death because I didn't tell my mom.

My inner guidance knew something was wrong, but I put it aside, and I trusted the adult.

This brief moment in time where I felt guided to say something to my mom, but didn't, had so many ripple effects in my life, and it took lots of work to unravel them all.

Another earlier memory follows.

I can remember a time in kindergarten where two girls were telling me that they were sisters.

I could feel that they were lying, but they weren't admitting they were lying.

I remember feeling conflicted. I knew I had to prove them wrong in order to validate what I was feeling.

I found out what their last names were, discovered they lived in adjacent houses, and they were still adamant that they were sisters.

They were just pretending, but it just compounded the issue. What I was experiencing was different than what others were telling me.

This is why I want you to forget about what's in your mind, and I want you to go back and remember what it felt like in that moment.

My inner guidance was actually right back then, wasn't it?

    There was something wrong with my grandad, right?

    They were actually friends, who were pretending to be sisters, right?

This is what I want you to recognize for yourself as this could be where you started to doubt or be uncertain of your own inner guidance.

The awareness that you were experiencing guidance, whether you followed it or not, is what I want you to bring into being.

Tune-In to your Inner Guidance Daily

Each and every day you are going to tune in to your inner guidance for a few minutes.

Just like you plug in your cell phone or laptop to recharge, you are going to learn to plug in your inner guidance system, and charge it.

Turn off your phone, and stop multitasking.

Uncross your legs, and open up your hands, palms up, ready to receive.

I want you to just think of something that makes you feel happy, really good, even joy!

Maybe, think about how great it would be to know that you can always trust your inner guidance. Notice the joy you would feel if you always knew you were being guided to your heart's desires.

Whatever it is that brings you happiness and joy, connect with that now, and repeat the words below out loud.

Remember, if you have a difficulty finding a joyful feeling and thought, look outside at nature or play a piece of music that will help open you to gratitude and a better feeling.

Tune-In: Palms up, Body open, Happy thought

I'm asking for my inner guidance

To clearly communicate with me,

In each and every moment,

For my highest and best good.

And I'm asking to be open to receive

This clear communication,

In each and every moment,

For my highest and best good.

And take joyful action on it.

Thank you!

Watch and Listen to how I do the Tune-In:

https://youtu.be/LNazErJFVgs

Stay with the feeling in your body for as long as you can. Notice what you are experiencing. Are your palms warm? Are you feeling cold? Do you have tingles? Are you feeling at peace? Do you feel pain anywhere? If so, speak it out. Release it. When you're done receiving, take your hands to your heart, as if you are closing the drawbridge to your castle. You are fully charged, protected, and ready for your day.

I am encouraging you to set forth the intention to connect with your inner guidance every morning.

It can be as simple as when you're getting out of bed, as soon as your feet hit the floor, stop, and open up.

Take a few minutes, and ask for your inner guidance to clearly communicate with you.

Set the intention that you're saying "clearly communicate with you, and that you are open to receiving it."

The truth is, your inner guidance is always communicating with you, but it's time for you to put your intention towards noticing it regularly. It's a gift that you have received to allow you to live in the NOW. It always knows what's best for you always in each moment.

Are you ready to open the gift fully and truly appreciate it?

This is your experience to discover your Superpower. Tune-In.

It's like tuning in to a radio station, the inner guidance radio station. The highest and best frequency for you at all times.

Tomorrow morning when you wake up, ask for the divine connection to your inner guidance, and be open to receiving the guidance.

It's that simple. If you don't believe it, have the 10 day experience and let your experience convince yourself.

If you read the section, "How to Use this Book for your Best Results," you are aware there is a private Facebook group. Many have shared their experiences, and encouraged others on their journeys too. If you choose to join, you can connect with others in Step 3 on each day.

Step 3: Watch and/or Listen to Awaken an Aha in You

Tina from USA

Gale from USA Day 1

Gale from USA Six months later

Day 2 of 10 - Your Body is Your Barometer

Did you do the Tune-In yet?

If not, let's do it. Only carry on reading after you have finished receiving the energy and being present to the words.

Step 1: Tune-In. Palms up, Body open, Happy thought

Say out loud:

I'm asking for my inner guidance

To clearly communicate with me,

In each and every moment,

For my highest and best good.

I'm asking to be open to receive

This clear communication,

In each and every moment,

For my highest and best good.

And to take joyful action on it.

Thank you!

The link below lets you do the energetic Tune-In with me.

https://youtu.be/LNazErJFVgs

When you have finished being present to the words you spoke, and receiving the energetic Tune-In, continue reading.

Do you feel the difference in opening and taking a minute or two just to get present to your inner guidance?

"How do I know when it's my inner guidance?" is a common question I am asked. I know you might want an easy answer. However, it's through your own personal experience that you will convince yourself of how your Superpower communicates with you, and leads you in the direction for your highest and best good.

Do you remember that I asked you to check everything that you actually know about the universe? Did you check them?

After all, how do you really know if any of it's true, until you let go of the past, and open to a new experience? Your inner guidance will lead you to the "don't know that you don't know" part of the Universe.

Everything is always changing, outside of yourself, in the Caterpillar World. There is nothing anyone can say that will ever affect your state of being when you are 100% convinced of your Superpower, Knowing what your inner guidance feels like to you is what the experience of these 10 days is about for you.

Your Body is Your Barometer

Your inner guidance is connected to everything, and is a vibrational frequency guiding you through your body.

Yes, your body, not your mind, is your barometer for your inner guidance.

For those of you who don't know what a barometer is, it's an instrument for measuring atmospheric pressure, used especially in forecasting the weather and determining altitude.

It is also defined as something that reflects changes in circumstances or opinions.

Your body is an instrument that tells you what does and doesn't feel good.

It gives you a heads up when you have no logical reason to feel that way. Animals trust their instincts, yet humans seem to second guess themselves, right?

Have you heard the saying, "trust your gut" or "what's your gut instinct?" The gut is part of your body, and if it is giving you a signal, do you notice it? Do you see how there can be a correlation to the growing concern about "gut health" and people's actual physical well being? If the gut is unhealthy it could be compromising the body's natural response to act as your barometer, don't you think? I explore this connection between gut health, overall health and your inner guidance in my group work.

Whatever it is that you believe about life, you are aware that you have a body that allows you to have an experience touching, tasting, seeing, smelling, hearing, and feeling. Consider it also contains your Superpower, and it's time to reset it so you can clearly follow it.

As I mentioned in Day 1, the heart is the pulse of your inner guidance. It's the connection to all that is on this planet. This is to give your mind a new reference point. Notice how it handles the idea. It might feel uncomfortable for your mind to trust your heart. Consider that the mind is more concerned about logic and control, and the heart is about love and connection. The gut is about having courage to act on what your heart is leading you to do. They are all in your body working in different ways.

As you continue to open to new ways of being, you can continue to expand your awareness of your truth as you define it. Your experience is your experience. Everyone will have their own experience.

Yes, I will repeat myself, **"Nothing matters except your experience."**

Notice what makes your body feel good today, and what makes your body feel stressed, anxious, or even just slightly uncomfortable.

Your inner guidance is always working for you.

For instance, if I go outside and I look at the trees, or I go to the ocean, or I walk barefoot, these are simple little things that I can do, and my body feels good.

You might be one of those people that getting off your feet and grabbing a cup of tea makes your body feel good.

Maybe it's having a bath, going for a massage, painting, singing, dancing, reading a good book, going for a jog, etc. that makes your body feel good.

Sometimes it might be yelling, "NO" that makes your body feel good. It's a release.

I have been known to get in the car with the windows up, and I let out a "AHHHHHH" for zero logical reason. I feel like I've just been overloaded by something, and it has to come out. A good yell for 10 seconds, and I'm brand new! I've released this invisible feeling that was bothering me.

When I say "good" I'm really asking you what makes you feel

relaxed, rejuvenated, revived, and reconnected. Are you in-joying this feeling in your body?

Whatever it is for you, it is different than it is for me, and probably everybody else.

We might like similar things, but each of us has preferences. It's all perfectly okay that we are different and unique.

When I go to the beach, I like to go barefoot, and feel the sand. I prefer walking at the ocean's edge, getting the best of the water and the feel of the sand. You may like to walk on the sand with sandals. Different preferences, make sense?

Step 2: Grab your notebook or open Notes, and answer the questions:

   Today notice in your body what brings you joy.

   What really brings you joy?

   How does your body feel in those moments?

   Is there an ease and a freedom?

   Do you smile from the inside out?

   Do your shoulders relax, and you breathe deeper?

   Are you more relaxed in Nature?

   Do you allow yourself to receive it?

   If not, why not?

For example, sometimes I like skipping through the parking lot.

I used to think people thought I was strange. I let go of that thought, and noticed as I skipped, a lot of them were smiling at my joy!

Now notice what your body feels like when you start to think of any situation that gives you stress. **Stress might be normal but it is not natural.**

Type A personalities are driven and push through their pain. They see it as a strength that they can endure the suffering and still produce results. "No pain. No gain." Then one day, they have a spontaneous health crisis, that forces them to approach life differently.

Some may use standard pharmacology, some may seek alternative or complementary therapies, and some may head to a mindfulness retreat. In all cases, this is the turning point for change, and is the start of them paying attention to their body. Wouldn't it be wonderful if you could pick up on the clues that your inner guidance is giving you about your body all the time?

What does your body feel when:

You listen to or watch the news?

Under the pressure of a deadline or going to be late?

Listening to someone who is always complaining about life?

When you watch a horror or dramatic movie?

When gossip is going on near you?

When you feel like someone is shaming, blaming you or wanting you to feel wrong?

I could go on and on. Even as I'm writing this, I am tightening up, feeling tense and stressed...how about you?

Does your body react in a constricted/restricted way?

Do you think the constricted/restricted way is beneficial to your immune system?

Many times as we feel tight and tense, we hear a dialog in our heads, "You will get through it. Move through that pain and discomfort. You can do it." There is some truth in that statement. All things do pass, but why is that pain or discomfort there? There is a pain that says STOP, and there is a discomfort that is **RESISTANCE** that leads to **BREAKTHROUGH**.

This is why it's important for you to understand what your body is communicating. There is a total difference between pain calling your attention to say NO, and resistance popping up when you are forming a new way of being. Leading to Breakthrough!

There is a fine difference, and it can be so slight that it is barely noticeable as you are beginning this journey. Then one day, you realize how easy it is to distinguish between STOP and plain resistance to your breakthrough and transformation.

NO is like a feeling in your body that communicates, "Don't go down that road."

Your body's putting on the brakes, similar to a car, and saying "stop, don't go in there, or don't do that, or stay away from that person or just cancel your plans." Does that make sense?

When you trust your inner guidance, you will know when you need to flee, versus being worried or anxious in that moment. There is a book by a security specialist, Gavin de Becker, *The Gift of Fear*, which explains that everyone received a sign before an attack happened. They just ignored it. Your heart, the pulse of your inner guidance is always communicating with you, beat by beat, and sending you signals.

Resistance is a different feeling. It represents that you are breaking through a habit that no longer serves you.

You are given an opportunity to go on a fabulous trip that you have been desiring, but your finances are lacking. You can feel this excitement, an opening occuring that wants to say yes. Your stomach feels like it's in knots because you are aware of your finances and there's no way you can see how this can happen.

You realize that there's an uneasiness in your body, but your tendency is to ignore it. It is communicating with you. It's wanting you to open to a new possibility.

You say NO based on your perception of your present circumstances. You have simply shut down the possibility of being guided to a new answer that you are unaware of in the "I don't know what I don't know" part of the Universe.

This is **RESISTANCE.** You feel a little bit of discomfort as you move through a new experience. Your mind is remembering the past. Your heart is giving you the signal to leave it behind and trust. It's directing you to move forward and have a new experience.

It's your job to understand what your body is really experiencing.

What is your Body Telling You?

Is it saying, "This is an opportunity", like a muscle stretching and getting stronger as you begin a new workout routine?

Or is it telling you, "No. Don't go there. Don't do it," and it feels like an abrupt stop or change of direction?

Two distinct feelings. Two distinct communications.

Your assignment is to discern the differences between **RESISTANCE and NO.**

As you are being more aware of your experiences today, write them down in your notebook or Notes, or record a video or audio to play back for yourself.

What is your body revealing to you?

Where are the sensations in your body, and what are they communicating to you?

If there is pain or dis-comfort ask it, "What do you want me to know?"

How do you handle the answers or feelings in your body?

Are you ignoring them?

Are you judging and rationalizing them?

Are you spending time understanding what is being communicated to you?

I remember when I first started to have these experiences that caused me to question every day experiences.

I'll use booking an appointment or committing to going to someone's house on a certain day, as an example.

The time would come for me to meet, and I would receive guidance to cancel at what seemed like the last minute, or not enough notice to be considerate.

My body would start to get agitated. I wanted to distract myself from what I was feeling.

My mind would be affected by all these thoughts:

"I've got to go there. I set this appointment. I've committed to it for a week or more now. It's linked to my calendar. What type of person would I be if I didn't show up for that appointment? Even if I called now, it's too late. I should have called earlier this morning to say that I can't make it. How will that look upon me, so I'd better go and save face."

I was experiencing this conflict. Subconscious habits and thoughts were popping up to keep me from being present to my body.

I learned in order to trust my Superpower, I had to do things or say things that seemed uncomfortable for me, even ridiculous at times, to receive the gift. In the beginning, I noticed that I wanted to lie, and make up some excuse that sounded good to keep up appearances, like, "Something came up…."

Then I discovered my body was getting uncomfortable at that idea, and was saying "NO you can't lie."

The more I did the daily energetic Tune-In, the more tuned in to my inner guidance I became. Then my inner guidance became so strong and loud, that I could NOT make up an excuse because I was aware of how agitated my body was if I did.

My inner guidance was getting stronger from all the recharging I was doing every day.

I started to say, "The truth is I will not be coming today. I'm just not feeling it."

You know what? My body was so relieved. At peace. Content. Happy.

I started to like this feeling of ease and less stress, and began to trust my Superpower more and more.

You know, that became my motto, "I'm just not feeling it."

If you ever saw the movie or read the book *He's Just Not That Into You*, well mine is "I'm just not feeling it".

Sometimes if the person was resisting my cancellation, I'd say, "If you want me to make up a story or make up an explanation of why I'm canceling, I can do that for you. The truth is that I'm feeling that it's not in my best good to come there now. I'm trusting that my inner guidance knows what's best for me and you."

What I discovered is when I actually followed through on the guidance, whether it was a one on one appointment for business or a personal commitment, I found it worked for them too.

Sometimes they didn't know it worked for them until after I cancelled.

I'd get a call later saying something like, "Remember I gave you a hard time about cancelling at the last minute? It's a good thing you did because…."

Sometimes, the other person was immediately relieved and grateful that I was cancelling. They may have needed the time for themselves but they wouldn't cancel because of their own desire to stay in integrity and honour their commitment.

Your inner guidance is connected to the bigger picture. Remember your heart is connected to Source / consciousness and is the pulse of your inner guidance. It knows if the other person is really stressed and needs that extra time for themselves.

Source / consciousness knows that the person was going to go ahead with the meeting anyways, because they felt responsible to be their word and do what's on the calendar.

Your inner guidance knows all this, because it's connected to Source / consciousness.

Living from your inner guidance is living in a world where you do not know the reasons why you are to cancel, but you follow it and trust the process.

Can you trust your Superpower and believe that you can enjoy your journey to your heart's desires? It will be new territory for you, and it's worth it!

That's why I'm here. I'm giving you the encouragement, to step out, and trust your Intuition/Inner Guidance, saying it's OK to have these experiences.

Convincing yourself of your amazing Superpower is what this is all about on these 10 days.

Get to know your body.

Become aware of the difference in sensations as you go about your day. Trust that your Body is Your Barometer. Your body will give you direction for your highest and best good.

It actually is irrelevant if you think you know everything about everything, if you are unaware of what your body is communicating with you.

Most people think stress is normal. Normal is different from Natural. Stress has an impact on your body. Consider that stress is caused because you are ignoring your inner guidance.

When you are stressed, you are resisting the natural flow and that directly impacts your body. It leads to dis-association, dis-order and even dis-ease, mentally and physically.

Consider that some of your present body pains may have been giving you signs for a course correction. Have you been noticing them or ignoring them?

My Experience

I had a history of eczema documented from the time I was two years old. I wasn't looking to get rid of it. I coped with it when it flared up on my body. It had actually been something I "owned" as if it was a part of me. Lots of people have health issues they live with, and one of mine was eczema.

I had done lots of cortisone, and other alternative & complementary therapies from positive affirmations to Chinese medicine. Symptoms eased and disappeared for a bit, but never healed.

In June 2009, I went to learn more about the teaching of Bruno Groening. I fell asleep with the first song that was played, so I really didn't know much of anything, except I felt guided to learn more at the end of that meeting. I liked this idea that there were people committed to following their divine guidance. It cost nothing to join the Circle of Friends, so I gave them my info.

They had a conference on Oct 31, 2009 which I felt guided to attend. I sat near the back of the room, palms up on my lap, ready to receive, and dozed on and off through the day. There were some pleasant stories shared, but it was a completely different experience to anything I had ever had in a group before.

It wasn't a praise God, hallelujah meeting, or an electric,

motivational, personal development seminar, or an out of this world meditation experience where I was communing with the Universe. It actually seemed uneventful, and boring hence why I dozed off.

I started the day with a bloody eczema rash on my chest. It had been there for weeks, and nothing that I had previously done had helped ease the itch and burning. There was a thought that my body was detoxing.

The morning after the conference, I awoke to discover my skin was perfectly baby soft. I kept looking at my chest throughout the day. I was wondering, "Am I seeing things? Is it going to come back? It's amazing, because I didn't do anything to make it disappear."

On that day, I knew this is what I had been asking for, but I was still in a state of dis-belief that it actually happened. It was a paradigm shift. I was down the rabbit hole, and I was determined to explore this until I was convinced that it was real for me, my family and everyone.

I've been completely free of all symptoms since that date, and consider myself healed.

As I look back on my life now, I feel that my eczema was a result of me feeling other sensations around me, and my body wanting to release this energy that was foreign to me. Our body is designed to release things in order to stay in health.

Are there symptoms or pains in your body that you have been told that you have to live with?

What if your body has a message for you? Are you listening? Are you ready to do something different?

As you go through your day, be aware of your body.

Notice:

> **What feels good and what doesn't feel good in your body?**
>
> **The explanations or the thoughts that come to you as you go about your day.**
>
> **Do you keep pushing yourself forward in a situation, where your body doesn't feel good?**
>
> **Do you stop allowing yourself to feel good?**
>
> **What you are noticing in your body?**

Write your discoveries in your notebook or Notes.

Speaking it or writing it out, releases the hold that some of these patterns have on you.

Sometimes when I write things down, I see another layer in the belief I was holding. Then I just let it go. Sometimes it is so ridiculous, I break out into laughter, and that's a great release.

I've learned to Tune-In and trust my Superpower as it is always tuned in for my highest and best good. My Body is my Barometer leading me to my heart's desires.

Now it's your time to convince yourself of your amazing Superpower.

If you just read the Tune-In at the beginning, but still haven't tuned in yet…do it now.

Tune-In: Palms up, Body open, Happy thought

Say out loud:

I'm asking for my inner guidance,

To clearly communicate with me,

For my highest and best good,

In each and every moment.

I'm asking to be open to receive.

This clear communication,

In each and every moment,

For my highest and best good.

And to take joyful action on it.

Thank you!

Stay with the feeling in your body for as long as you can. Notice what you are experiencing. Are your palms warm? Are you feeling cold? Do you have tingles? Are you feeling at peace? Do you feel pain anywhere? If so, speak it out. Release it. When you're done receiving, take your hands to your heart, as if you are closing the drawbridge to your castle. You are fully charged, protected, and ready for your day.

Tune-In with ME

https://youtu.be/LNazErJFVgs

Take notice of what you experience, write it down, or share what you're willing to share in the private Facebook group. Share with us about what makes you feel good, or what you noticed that makes you feel awful, maybe even sick to your stomach. Maybe you realized something today about your body that you've been ignoring.

Step 3: Watch and/or Listen to Awaken an Aha in You

Mena from Portugal

Maria from England

Day 3 of 10 - Receiving Thoughts

Did you do the Tune-In yet?

If not, let's do it. Only carry on reading after you have finished receiving the energy and being present to the words.

Step 1: Tune-In: Palms up, Body open, Happy thought

Say out loud:

I'm asking for my inner guidance

To clearly communicate with me,

In each and every moment,

For my highest and best good.

And I'm asking to be open to receive

This clear communication,

In each and every moment,

For my highest and best good.

And take joyful action on it.

Thank you!

The link below lets you do the energetic Tune-In with me.

https://youtu.be/LNazErJFVgs

When you have finished being present to the words you spoke, and receiving the energetic Tune-In, continue reading.

Do you feel the difference in opening and taking a minute or two

just to get present to your inner guidance?

I am excited for today, this is probably going to be a new conversation for most of you.

Remember I asked you to take everything that you know and put it aside for 10 days while you're having this experience? The reason is because it's about your experience. It's through your own experiences that you will move from believing and hoping to discovering and convincing yourself of the Superpower that lives in you at all times....your Intuition/Inner Guidance.

Day 1 was to really write out what you believe about your intuition/inner guidance, to give you an idea of what is the foundation for yourself of what you believe, how it works, etc.

Day 2 was about starting to look at your body as your barometer and noticing how it is guiding you.

On Day 3 I'm going to be talking about this lovely head of yours, and this idea that you've been taught that you're thinking thoughts. Your mind is telling you things, and pulling you away from your inner guidance at times.

Receiving Thoughts

I want you to consider, that you actually are a receiver. Yes. You are a receiver, like a radio station or a cell tower receives a signal. You too, receive a signal. You receive thoughts. Thoughts are forces. Thoughts are vibrations. Thoughts affect everyone in different ways.

You get to choose if you want to listen to that thought, or you get to choose if you want to turn the station. You get to choose if you want to read a text message or delete it. You get to choose to accept a DM or delete it. I know it's tempting because it showed up on your phone or in your inbox, right? Do you keep reading a direct message over and over again that bothers you or do you trash it?

Almost 10 years ago, when my daughters first started tuning into healing energy daily, I noticed that they started to hear things differently. They started to turn off the radio station that they were listening to because they could sense that that vibration was bothering them.

The station that they used to listen to was being changed to a more easy rock station or just turned off completely. They started saying that it didn't feel so good; which amazed me as they always had music on in the background. They changed the station.

It's like they became more in tune. It's like singing. We can all sing. Some of us sing really well. Some of us, just okay, and some people are lucky enough to have perfect pitch.

That's the idea of fine tuning your vibration. The more you work on fine tuning your vibration, the clearer your tone becomes. The easier it is to hear and be present. The faster you are able to release the vibration.

This is how it is with your thoughts. You have vibrations and frequencies all around you. Everyone is impacted differently. Some love the sound of classical music or opera where others run and hide.

Chances are that you have been believing most of what you were taught to think during your school years. In fact, you have come to accept it as Truth. It's like you have taken ownership of these ideas.

It's just become true for you, right?

If you go back in time to when you were born, you were receiving things that your parents were saying.

Everybody was cooing over the baby, "Oh, you're so beautiful." "You are so amazing!" Some people were saying, "She's got her mother's eyes, or her father's nose."

You were absorbing all these thoughts around you like a sponge, right? You've heard that saying, "You're like a sponge."

You're receiving all this. You're still receiving things. You're receiving things from the media. You're receiving things from experts online. You're receiving this communication from me.

What I'm encouraging you to do is feel within yourself; to discern. Does this feel authentic for you? Does this communication feel good in your body? If you have pain in your body, do you talk to it, or do you medicate it?

When you discover the amazingness of your Superpower, your inner guidance, there is this sense within you, an inner peace, and a confidence that all is perfectly fine.

When everybody else is going left, you're saying, "Nope. Not for me, it's right." You're confident in that guidance.

Trusting your guidance is truly the most amazing gift you can give yourself. It is a sense of freedom. Freedom from everything else around you. Freedom from every opinion and conversation outside yourself.

Step 2: Grab your notebook or open Notes, and answer the questions

As you go about your day, be aware of how you are being affected by your thoughts.

How is your body affected by thoughts you are receiving today?

Is your body feeling good?

If you start to feel negatively affected by these thoughts that you're receiving, why do you want to keep listening to them?

What's the payoff for you to keep listening to them?

What's the benefit to you to feel anything less than joy in your body?

Simple questions, yet the answers that you discover about yourself could be quite deep.

Take a walk. Reground yourself or reconnect yourself with nature. Take a moment to consciously notice your breath. Do whatever it is you need to do. It's important to get yourself back in authentic alignment, so you can really pay attention to what you are experiencing.

The other way I'm going to say this to you, is to take you way back to when computers had a big external hard drive. Remember those old PC's that came out in the eighties?

They had a hard-drive, an external floppy drive, and there was a separate monitor. Each PC was completely separate from everyone else's computer. You have been told that you are like the PC. You work as well as the input or software that was installed...that you received. You were outputting, based on the input, right?

Now, we have this wonderful world, that is a physical manifestation of what's really going on in the universe. We call it the Internet. We call it cloud computing. We are constantly upgrading our software. If you've got a iPhone, you know it seemed like yesterday that you did the IOS 10.1 update, and now you are getting a message to do IOS 10.3

If you have an older phone, you are realizing that your phone can't do some of the new apps because it's out of date.

The new software needs more memory to work. The new software has many more applications that can be used. You can get by for so long on the old software, and then your things are just archaic. That's how the world is now.

You can keep believing all the things you were taught. Keep knowing that you think you know everything, but everything is changing. Everything is rapidly shifting in the universe, as you keep vibrating and upping your frequency to more authentic truths, you will see it and experience it.

Once you update your software, it says right in the terms and conditions, you can't go back and some things may never work the same way as you were used to before the update, right?

You hit the button and accept, the process of updating begins, and then it's complete and ready for you to experience. Today, it's all about accepting the software update, called, "You actually do receive thoughts and energetic vibrations constantly."

Are you willing to receive it?

Notice the messages that you are receiving and listening to today.

Do you want to listen to them? Or do you resist or ignore them?

Are you feeling joy, contentment or an opening in your body?

Does that thought make you feel anxious, resentful, bothered or constricted/restricted in your body?

Treat the thought that you are receiving as if it is from a person that was always sharing doubt and uncertainty, and everything negative with you.

Do you keep listening to that person? Do you walk away? Shake it off? Pretend it doesn't bother you? Get frustrated? Irritated? Resentful?

What is your body feeling as you are receiving thoughts, and how it is affecting you moment by moment?

What's the impact on you and others, by carrying those feelings forward in your day?

This is why you're here, to have an experience, so you can discover your Superpower and convince yourself of what is true.

My Experience

My former husband said to me, "Pick me or the Circle of Friends." Essentially he was asking me to choose him over my personal spiritual experience. When I tuned in, I heard "pick him." I felt "tightness in my stomach" like I was going to throw up at that idea.

Why would I want to give up that intuitive spiritual connection that was responsible for help and healings in me and around me?

The day before, my eldest had contacted me from Sweden as she was touring with her choir, and was feeling ill. They didn't know what to do for her, as I had never given her pharmaceutical medicine. I immediately contacted a few of my friends, who tuned in for her, and within an hour she was all good.

Again I asked myself the question, "Why would I want to give up that type of connection and power to help others come back to health for him? Especially since we had been having challenges in our marriage throughout our 15 years together."

I tuned in three times, and all three times I heard one thing and felt another. This was a new experience for me, so I reached out to a dear friend, to say I need help with getting clarity. We tuned in together. I've learned that when one or more tunes in together, the inner guidance system hears more clearly. This is especially true while one is discovering and strengthening their Superpower.

In that moment, a complete calm came over me through my body. The message was to choose the Circle of Friends. The other thought I was hearing was gone. Nothing changed in our relationship based on that choice, but it was the beginning of our final chapter together. I knew to rely on my body, the barometer, versus a voice outside of my head. It was an important experience for me to trust what I was feeling versus the words I was hearing.

Write what you're noticing in your notebook or open up Notes on your phone as these experiences happen during your day, so you will remember.

That's the scoop for today!

If you just read the Tune-In at the beginning of this chapter, and still haven't tuned in yet…do it now.

Tune-In: Palms up, Body open, Happy thought

I'm asking for my inner guidance,

To clearly communicate with me,

In each and every moment,

For my highest and best good.

I'm asking to be open to receive,

This clear communication,

In each and every moment,

For my highest and best good.

And take joyful action on it.

Thank you!

Stay with the feeling in your body for as long as you can. Notice what you are experiencing. Are your palms warm? Are you feeling cold? Do you have tingles? Are you feeling at peace? Do you feel pain anywhere? If so, speak it out. Release it. When you're done receiving, take your hands to your heart, as if you are closing the drawbridge to your castle. You are fully charged, protected, and ready for your day.

Tune-In with ME:

https://youtu.be/LNazErJFVgs

As people share in the private Facebook group, others are seeing things about themselves, and others are going, "Aha. I've done that too." Or, "Yes, I've had a similar experience, and didn't see it that way."

We've all had experiences. The more we share the experiences that we have, and what we also noticed, we are helping each other. We learn from each other.

You have to be a member of the private Facebook group to listen, and it's a great gift to yourself to connect with others.

Step 3: Watch and/or Listen to Awaken an Aha in You

Kate from England

Carolyne from Indonesia

Day 4 of 10 - Trust the Timing

Did you do the Tune-In yet?

If not, let's do it. Only carry on reading after you have finished receiving the energy and being present to the words.

Step 1: Tune-In: Palms up, Body open, Happy thought

Say out loud:

I'm asking for my inner guidance,

To clearly communicate with me,

In each and every moment,

For my highest and best good.

And I'm asking to be open to receive

This clear communication,

In each and every moment,

For my highest and best good.

And take joyful action on it.

Thank you!

The link below lets you do the energetic Tune-In with me.

https://youtu.be/LNazErJFVgs

When you have finished being present to the words you spoke, and receiving the energetic Tune-In, continue reading.

Do you feel the difference in opening and taking a minute or two

just to get present to your inner guidance?

Yeah! You have made it to Day 4. You are being awesome at learning to trust your intuition/inner guidance. In fact, you are just plain awesome! I am the sparkler to ignite your inner guidance.

I do hope you are doing the Tune-In with me daily, writing in your notebook or Notes, and being honest with yourself about what you are noticing. Embrace all your new awareness.

If you are the type of person that thinks that reading the book will give you the gift of trusting your inner guidance, you are mistaken. **Knowing is doing**. If you put your intention towards noticing yourexperience, you will gain more awareness. Through this experience, you will discover and convince yourself of your own Superpower. It will always lead you to your highest and best good.

Step 2: Grab your notebook or open Notes, and answer the questions

Now is the time to start to practice the first three basics.

Day 1 was about writing in your notebook or Notes, what you actually believe about your inner guidance system. This gave you a starting point and a foundational perspective to begin your experiential journey.

Have you noticed any shifts in your perceptions in these three days from what you wrote? Write them down.

Are you doing the Tune-In each day with ME?

Day 2 was to experience your body as your barometer.

I asked you to become more aware that your body has a feeling of moving you forward or holding you back at different times. What brings you joy and expansion? What is causing you to constrict/restrict and limit yourself?

What experiences in your body have you observed and been able to identify and differentiate?

Day 3 I asked you to consider that your body is like a receiver, and that you are actually receiving thoughts vs thinking thoughts.

Many who have taken the time to be with this concept have found a new freedom of choice to turn the channel or delete a message. Did you? Or are you still contemplating the idea, that was taught to you, that your brain thinks thoughts?

This is why it's so important for you to really be aware of your experiences and convince yourself through your body.

Are you a thinker or a receiver?

Are these thoughts or ideas yours?

Is that thought feeling good in your body?

Have you absorbed a thought that you repeat without even being aware what you are really saying or feeling?

For instance, the idea that has been spread like a virus, that individuals repeat, "Oh it's my monkey mind!" Seriously do you have a monkey mind? Does repeating that phrase empower you or affirm that you feel like your mind operates on it's own and you are powerless to the random thoughts?

No! Turn it off. Disconnect it.

Change the channel. Delete the message.

Imagine you are listening to a video, a Facebook live, a podcast, and you don't like it.

Do you keep listening or do you disconnect?

If you notice that you are feeling irritated or agitated, why do you keep listening?

What's the payoff?

Do you know Dr. Emoto's work? He placed words like Love and Hate on the outside of a container of water. When he analyzed the water crystals, Love created a beautiful, majestic water crystal. Hate turned the water to sludge. Imagine what the thoughts you are receiving and entertaining are doing to your body?

Trust the Timing

Day 4 is about you waking up with your day planned.

You probably have a to do list and your day is already to happen.

The question I want you to ponder is:

Is everything and everywhere that you have planned in your highest and best good today?

Notice what thoughts come to you as you tune in to your guidance.

You might be saying, "What? I have all this stuff planned. Of course I have to do it."

Remember my experiences I shared as I started to follow cancelling appointments?

The magic happens when you can learn to trust your inner guidance and the universe to work in all areas of your life and for others too.

Isn't that what you want? For your life to easily flow, granting all your heart's desires?

Let's say, you actually woke up today, with a huge to do list and you have it all planned out.

You do your quick morning Tune-In.

You discover that it is truly the most extraordinary day, and your heart's desire is to go take a walk in the forest, or be by the beach, or to be by yourself for awhile in nature or in the bath.

It could be sitting looking at nature from your car, taking time to have a coffee or enjoying a cup of tea, or by a fire reading one chapter of this book!

Your heart is saying, "Yes! Go play in nature!" You are receiving, "No, you can't because you have all this to do?" Stop and ask:

"Inner Guidance, I'm asking you to clearly communicate with me. Is this for my highest and best good?" Follow what you receive.

The answer you receive is "Do both." Immediately your mind says, "I can't do both. I don't have enough time." What are you ultimately saying about Source / consciousness if you think it's impossible to give you enough time to do both?

Do you see how you have limited the entire universe?

Your mind can't conceive of how it's possible. Your inner guidance knows how, but the only way you will know is to have the experience.

Trusting the Timing Examples

My daughter was saying that she had been listening to a radio station, and they were hosting a special Halloween party.

She was wondering if she should contact them about donating tickets to the food bank as part of the gifts that could be given out to whomever raised the most food.

She had received this thought that this radio station had these tickets, right?

She was wondering, receiving thoughts, if she should contact them or when she should contact them? A few days passed.

Then one morning, she got the thought to listen to the station. At that moment, they said call in with a scary story to win tickets.

She also received the thought, "You are never going to get through."

She ignored the doubting thought, because she felt like this was her moment to call, and followed through on her inner guidance.

She called. It rang once, and they picked up the phone,

They heard her story, and liked it. They gave her four tickets, two more than they were giving out. This unexpected gift of two additional tickets met her secret heart desire to go to the Radio Halloween party.

Now she had two tickets to donate to the prizes for the food bank Halloween for Hunger event that she was coordinating, and two tickets for herself.

Inner guidance happens like that when you're in the moment.

Another time, I had an issue with my car, when we first came to

Prince Edward Island (PEI). I was wondering who to trust, who knew where to go, what station, what maintenance place would be the best etc.

I tuned in, and I asked my inner guidance, "what do I do?"

I received the name of someone that I had met over the summer.

I asked my inner guidance, "Do I call him now?" I received, "No."

I went on with my day. The next day I tuned in, and asked, and the answer was no again.

On the third day, it was, "Yes, call him now." He answered immediately

He told me to pull into the McDonald's parking lot as I was driving into town, and he would be right there. Sure enough, in about 30 seconds, his truck pulled in. He had just left the hardware store down the street.

He checked the car in the parking lot, and discovered the bolt in the oil pan was cracked, and ordered me a new bolt that I could pick up immediately.

I picked up the part, and as I pulled into his driveway, I heard this thump. The car fell to the driver's side perfectly placed in his driveway. Exactly where he would fix the car.

He looked at the car and saw that the ball joint of the car had broken off. He and his friend stood there flabbergasted at the perfection of it.

"Whoa, who is looking out for you? Most people's ball joints break on the highway, and they spin off into the ditch. They lose control or they hit another car. There is never a safe place for a ball joint to break."

"For your ball joint to break right here in my driveway, right where I would fix the car...well ...that's just unheard of."

Now here's the other part of that story that happened before I discovered the leak.

About three weeks prior I was told that my ball joint was loose. I tuned in to ask if I was to fix it now. I received, "No." I had just turned a corner very quickly and the car was fine.

I then drove the car from Toronto to PEI about 1800 kms, and 100 km of highway driving each day for 11 days before it finally broke down in the perfect spot to be fixed.

He fixed it within a couple hours at a fabulous price.

When you're in the right timing, everything works, and that is all related to your inner guidance as it's connected to the Source of the Universe.

Here's what I learned about that encounter months later. I had shared with him about the teaching of Bruno Groning, which is to give away your ailment, turn around and trust God is healing you. He followed my instructions and gave away his anxiety. He opened up to receive the gift of health. He had a healing. He never took any anxiety medication again, and began healing on all levels from the inside out.

Following your inner guidance provides gifts and blessings for other people too. We are all connected in a magical, illogical way, that the heart knows intimately. It's fun once you get comfortable living out of your comfort zone and in the inner guidance zone! It truly is a whole new world!

Today ask if each item on your to-do list is for your highest and best good?

Notice what your body's feeling in that minute that you Tune-In.

Notice if you Trust Your Guidance or have some resistance to following the guidance.

This exercise today and your experiences can open up many gifts and blessings for you in your life. Notice what you notice, and write it down.

If you just read the Tune-In at the beginning of this chapter, and still haven't tuned in yet…do it now.

Tune-In: Palms up, Body open, Happy thought

I'm asking for my inner guidance,

To clearly communicate with me,

In each and every moment,

For my highest and best good.

I'm asking to be open to receive,

This clear communication,

In each and every moment,

For my highest and best good.

And take joyful action on it.

Thank you!

Stay with the feeling in your body for as long as you can. Notice what you are experiencing. Are your palms warm? Are you feeling cold? Do you have tingles? Are you feeling at peace? Do you feel pain anywhere? If so, speak it out. Release it. When you're done receiving, take your hands to your heart, as if you are closing the drawbridge to your castle. You are fully charged, protected, and ready for your day!

Tune-In with ME

https://youtu.be/LNazErJFVgs

Step 3: Watch and/or Listen to Awaken an Aha in You

It is fun to see the "Aha's" that have been posted in the private Facebook group as each has their own experience. If you haven't joined, you may want to and have the experience of the community there. (If you don't do Facebook, you can be like I was in 2016, when I created an account to only participate in a group).

Tina from USA

Neltah from Ireland

DAY 5 OF 10 - YOUR STORY

Did you do the Tune-In yet?

If not, let's do it. Only carry on reading after you have finished receiving the energy and being present to the words.

Step 1: Tune-In. Palms up, Body open, Happy thought

Say out loud:

I'm asking for my inner guidance,

To clearly communicate with me,

In each and every moment,

For my highest and best good.

I'm asking to be open to receive

This clear communication,

In each and every moment,

For my highest and best good.

And to take joyful action on it.

Thank you!

The link below lets you do the energetic Tune-In with me.

https://youtu.be/LNazErJFVgs

When you have finished being present to the words you spoke, and receiving the energetic Tune-In, continue reading.

Do you feel the difference in opening and taking a minute or two

just to get present to your inner guidance?

This is Day 5, and you are halfway through Trusting Your Intuition - Discover Your Superpower in 10 days. Numerologists will say that the number five is about transformation and change. Consider that you are halfway through yours, and there could be some shifts going on.

You may have started to get some "Ahas." You may have become more aware about what you're experiencing. You may have discovered that your body has some sensations, that maybe you were led to go here or maybe you weren't. You're discovering the Superpower that you have as your Inner Guidance.

You have been experimenting with the idea that you get to choose whether or not to accept a thought or turn it off. Changing the channel gives your different results. It's amazing, isn't it?

Imagine if you can just change the channel on that thought on "time" and say, "There's always enough time." How would that affect your life?

Man made up the idea of time. It is an illusion. Even Einstein questioned the idea of time and matter before his passing, suggesting that it was flexible. How about listening to, "I choose there's always enough time?" I've learned to be patient and trust the timing of my inner guidance.

What's Your Story?

Everyone has a story. "Your Story" is about you and your life. It's relevant to your inner guidance because you have a story that affects how you interpret your experience.

Even though I've asked you to check everything that you know about the Universe etc., you still have ideas, beliefs, and phrases that are derived from Your Story. This affects your perception of your experience, and shows up in the ways you share about your experiences.

Although you think you did check things, you are still being impacted by Your Story.

It has payoffs and rewards for you. You can justify it, rationalize it, and even offer proof based on your perceptions of your experiences. Your Story supports you in being right where you are now. For instance, I used to believe for decades:

"Life was like an onion, and I had to continually peel layers, and peel the layers."

I was always going to be working through things. It was a given that this was an ongoing journey, and I was never going to be done on this journey. It was tiring always looking and working on myself.

When I was in My Story of peeling the onion layers, I was living My Story. I certainly didn't believe that I could just be completely free. I really believed I had to keep peeling the onion layers. I always had to be doing something to find that inner peace. It was a constant process releasing patterns. I was looking at a situation, analyzing, realizing, "Once again it must be me, because I didn't get the outcome I wanted."

The payoff was that I could feel good about myself because I was taking personal responsibility for my health and well being, and striving to be better all the time. As I was unravelling the layers, I was affecting generations…. as the story goes!

Now, I believe that was such a sales pitch. Yes, you read it correctly. A sales pitch.

The amount of money that people have spent on personal development, spiritual awakening, mental and emotional wellness, in order to get present to what we already have been given, is outstanding. About ½ billion dollars a year!

It's mesmerizing when you become aware of the idea that we have to DO something to get to BE. We are paying for something we already have, but we have forgotten to tap in and use our inner guidance to enjoy the journey of our heart's desires.

It's like we have been hypnotized into a deep slumber, like a slowly moving caterpillar, that only allows us to only hear other people's suggestions. We have forgotten about our own Superpower and how beneficial it is to each of us. It's always with us, and patiently waiting to be rediscovered so you can turn up it's volume.

Upon discovery, it's like we move into the chrysalis, where listening becomes easier. Our Superpower becomes activated and our attention starts to go toward our feelings, our heart, and less towards the mind. Then one day, you realize you really are becoming a butterfly, leaving your old ways behind. You wonder, "Why did I take so long to trust what was being communicated to me!"

When you have confidence in your inner guidance, then you can smile, and love others when they give their opinion, and keep going where you are led to go. You can trust the process for everyone.

Step 2: Grab your notebook or open Notes, and answer the questions

You need to be OK with Your Story, and see how it's working for you. Write Your Story. Better yet, record an audio or video of Your Story, and then play it back listening to yourself, and notice what you feel or the thoughts that you receive.

Your Story could be like one of these:

Life is about peeling onion layers.

I always self sabotage myself.

I work hard on changing but it never really works.

I have committed to this or gave my word, so I have to follow through.

I wish I could, but I just don't have the money.

I've tried new things and I was wrong, so how do I know this is right?

I am always struggling with something. I have to live with it as the doctor has done everything possible.

I still have to deal with these things first and then I can…. I have to work until the kids get through college, and then I can have a life. I inherited this …… from my parents so there's nothing I can do about it.

I have a bad memory or a monkey mind.

Can't teach an old dog new tricks.

I knew it wouldn't work.

I follow whatever my spirit guide, angel or guru says.

I don't really believe I'm worthy to have what I want.

How does your body feel when you identify with Your Story?

Do you feel joy?

Are you noticing that your body is constricting/restricting as you listen to yourself?

Write down what you are noticing in your body related to Your Story.

Remember on Day 2, Your Body is Your Barometer, you learned that stress is normal but not natural.

Stress is so normal there have been studies that people have done to tell you how to let go of your stress. There has been lots of information on what brings about your stress, how to overcome your stress, and do things differently. Take everything you've ever learned about stress, just put it to the side for now.

Consider that you're doing something that is causing you stress. Why are you choosing to continue doing it? What's the payoff to your body and Your Story?

Day 3 you learned how to change the channel, when you keep receiving those same thoughts that bother you.

Do you keep listening to Your Story as truth?

Are you 100% sure there isn't a possibility that you could be wrong?

Can you open to that tiny possibility that things can change for the good?

Day 4 you learned to open up and you ask your inner guidance about the activities in your day. Some of you wanted to go play, but Your Story was so strong or ingrained in you, that you were unable to follow your inner guidance.

Will Your Story let you follow your inner guidance and enjoy your life?

Does Your Story keep you peeling onion layers?

Are you looking for the "why" of the experience and searching for answers.

When you input keywords or a questions into Google or another search engine, you get answers based on your question, right? The quality of your answer depends on your question. Searching for a "why" something is happening gets you different results than entering key words in the direction you wish to go.

Is it Really Your Story or are Others the Authors of Your Story?

I believe every child starts out in this world feeling like all their heart's desires can come true, and then they get hypnotized into forgetting who they are and why they are here.

Science has shown that children generally live in Alpha and Theta brain waves until the age of 7. In this state, there is no critical thinking, no questioning. The best way to describe the state is they are in a hypnotic or meditative trance. Hence the saying "Children are like a sponge." They identify with the world around them as them. They believe what others are saying, and absorb all those thoughts and make them into what is now Your Story.

Your Story is a book of beliefs that you were given mainly by others. You absorbed it. You inherited it from your parents, your teachers, the books you read, the shows you watched, the media and the world outside of yourself.

Did you get told you were like your mom, dad, or any other family members?

Many people repeat phrases they have heard like, "I'm just like my mom or dad." When I ask them if they like their parents, they will say, "No, not everything."

My next question is, "How do you feel in your body, when you are present to those words?" Usually the person discovers a feeling in their body, dis-comfort, pain, tension that until that moment they were unaware they were carrying around with that belief.

Are you feeling any inner conflict in your body with Your Story?

Do you believe that Your Story is 100% true?

Can you see the limitations of Your Story on the journey to your heart's desires?

Does your story keep you living in joy, health, peace, love and wealth?

Is it possible Your Story could be rewritten?

Know that Your Story is a book of beliefs from the past that you can close and say, "I'm done with it."

Open up to receive the TRUTH of your inner guidance.

A New Story

How does it feel to say, "I have this feeling inside me that I can have a great life now. I have to trust my inner guidance knows what's best for me, one step at a time"?

Do you believe that you can have a New Story that supports you to have time for yourself and still get everything done in perfect timing?

For me My Original Story was, "Work hard, make lots of money, and have freedom."

My New Story after returning from Africa was, "Never participate in what most people call the real world again."

The New Story led me to be healed from eczema, yeast infections, depression, bulimia, abdominal migraines, constipation, and narcolepsy. However that was never my intention. I still felt these health issues were "Normal." Only later did I realize **Normal isn't natural**. I'll write more about that journey on Day 6.

One day, you will be amazed at how you never repeat Your Original Story the same way anymore at all…..EVER! It can be totally and completely forgotten, like moving from a caterpillar to a butterfly.

I can totally attest to this, as I have almost completely forgotten how challenging my life was when I had narcolepsy. This was the caterpillar stage of my life, as part of My Original Story was that my body was a victim to outside forces. I was helpless and powerless if the doctor couldn't help me with pharmaceutical drugs.

It was only through reading the narcolepsy support group on Facebook recently, that I remembered all the things that I used to have to deal with every day. I had completely forgotten and had such compassion for myself for what I lived through. As a butterfly. I know my health comes from healing from the inside out. I'm so glad my Superpower always knows what's best for me, and consistently leads me to my heart's desires better than I ever imagined!

This is what happens when you are discovering your Superpower, and are led to a whole new world...your Best Whole New World. You become present to the gift of NOW, which is located in the **don't know, what you don't know** part of the Universe.

It begins with you having decided that you are done with Your Story in the Caterpillar World. You enter into the Chrysalis of Transformation. In the Chrysalis, it's like you go back and forth between Your Original Story and Your New Story. When you are completely convinced that your wings are strong enough, you break open the chrysalis, and fly to new magical heights. You have become a Butterfly.

As a Butterfly you realize that Your Story is irrelevant. It's Surrender - the Ultimate Trust. Surrender comes after lots and lots of experiences of trusting your own intuition/inner guidance. It's embracing LIFE in a whole new way. It's living in the NOW.

I have given you a lot to consider here. Take the time you need to consider if you are 100% sure Your Story is TRUTH, or if it's time you let go of some of the beliefs you have absorbed. It really is all about a choice. Keep Your Original Story or create Your New Story?

Did you do your Tune-In?

If you just read the Tune-In at the beginning of this chapter, and still haven't tuned in yet...do it now.

Tune-In: Palms up, Body open, Happy thought

I'm asking for my inner guidance,

To clearly communicate with me,

In each and every moment,

For my highest and best good.

I'm asking to be open to receive,

This clear communication,

In each and every moment,

For my highest and best good.

And take joyful action on it.

Thank you!

Stay with the feeling in your body for as long as you can. Notice what you are experiencing. Are your palms warm? Are you feeling cold? Do you have tingles? Are you feeling at peace? Do you feel pain anywhere? If so, speak it out. Release it. When you're done receiving, take your hands to your heart, as if you are closing the drawbridge to your castle. You are fully charged, protected, and ready for your day!

Tune-In with ME

https://youtu.be/LNazErJFVgs

You may find this is a good time to join the private Facebook group if you haven't yet, as everybody explains how this experience is occurring for them a little differently.

Step 3: Watch and/or Listen to Awaken an Aha in You

Brenda from Ireland

Carolyne from Indonesia

DAY 6 OF 10 - TWO MAIN BROADCASTS

Did you do the Tune-In yet?

If not, let's do it. Only carry on reading after you have finished receiving the energy and being present to the words.

Step 1: Tune-In. Palms up, Body open, Happy thought

Say out loud:

I'm asking for my inner guidance,

To clearly communicate with me,

In each and every moment,

For my highest and best good.

I'm asking to be open to receive

This clear communication,

In each and every moment,

For my highest and best good.

And to take joyful action on it.

Thank you!

The link below lets you do the energetic Tune-In with me.

https://youtu.be/3FM-P7aM2FQ

When you have finished being present to the words you spoke, and receiving the energetic Tune-In, continue reading.

Do you feel the difference in opening and taking a minute or two

just to get present to your inner guidance?

I hope you took the necessary time to see, write, and become aware of Your Story and how it has impacted your life previously.

Are you ready for the next idea to consider as you Learn to Trust Your Inner Guidance?

This one is really key. It will move you from your mind to your heart if you take it all in.

Two Main Broadcasts

I want you to consider that there are two main broadcasts going on in our perceived world.

Some will say it is God and the devil. Some will say it's light and shadow. Some will say yin and yang. Some will say that it's love and fear. Others will say it's consciousness and ego, right?

There always seems to be two main ways to describe or discern the experience that we have called life. This is what we have been led to call duality.

There was ONE before there became two.

I want you to go back in time, and consider that there was something in the beginning. Something created the Big Bang. Something began this whole process of "life." I've identified this as God growing up. I have also called this something, Source, Creator, Universal Intelligence, Divine Intelligence, IT or ONE.

Source / consciousness created everything you need. One presence that created what you call the Universe, Earth, Nature, Animals, Plants, Reptiles and Humanity. Consider this creation is similar to a programmer creating a video game full of infinite possibilities.

Source / consciousness also created Joy, Health, Love, Peace, and Wealth. Even Freedom, Kindness, Harmony, Compassion and Infinite possibilities are always there.

Remember your heart is the pulse of your inner guidance and is connected to Source / consciousness. It is your unique GPS guiding you to have wonderful, fabulous experiences that are consistent with your heart's desires.

The other broadcast is sending out thoughts and ideas that are Deceptive and distracting from your connection to Source / consciousness. Creating an illusion or mirage that becomes normal or considered to be "real life."

The Deceptive broadcast has most people convinced that suffering, doubts, stress, lack, limitation, shame, blame, guilt, fear, dis-ease, dis-order, anxiety, fear, and more are "real life."

Think about a child. They enjoy playing with blocks, building sandcastles, tumbling in the grass, playing with your cell phone, and enjoying the process of living in the moment. They wake up each morning with enthusiasm for the day.

Somewhere in Your Story, you were taught to stop being in the experience, for the sake of the experience. You were given ideas about "real life." There started to be goals, a destination, a plan to become someone or make something of yourself. Generally people are taught that the only achievement is through hard work.

If you knew that you were being deceived, would you keep doing what you are doing? Maybe as a child you had no option but to play along with the deception, but as an adult you do have a choice.

Would you rather live in the moment enjoying playing with

each experience, or do the same thing over and over again and expect a different result?

Your inner guidance is connected to Source / consciousness, and the other Deceptive broadcast contains the Library of everyones' stories. There are many stories, books, volumes, in each area of the library validating the deceptive broadcast.

The job of the Deceptive broadcast is to run interference with your inner guidance, and be like a decoy, so you are unaware what is truly being communicated to you at all times. This concept of two broadcasts is like duality and exists all the time. You have the ability to choose what to listen to and follow in every single moment.

Today, become aware that every single moment has a space.

It is in that space, we experience the two main broadcasts

Become aware which main broadcast has your attention: Deception or Inner Guidance?

Step 2: Grab you Notebook of Notes. Start writing the answers

When you get up in the morning, you are awake from your sleeping stage, but are you AWAKE?

Essentially there have been many messages throughout history, to wake us up from the dream of separation. Every great master, over thousands of years, has expressed TRUTH in their own unique way, channeled from Source / consciousness directly.

Ekhart Tolle's book, A New Earth, was written more than 10 years ago and it was about awakening, yet people still aren't awake.

What if you decide today to become AWAKE and trust your inner guidance?

What if awakening is about you trusting and believing that the outcome will be for your highest and best good always?

What if you can receive exactly what you need from this omnipresence that exists and has always existed, at any given moment in time?

Are you ready:

> **To take a step forward in trusting and believing in a whole new world?**

> **To lift the veil of deception, and AWAKEN to what's always been there?**

Consider that being AWAKE is being present, and you are capable of choosing what's best for you which is always your inner guidance.

You get to choose in the next moment. You get to decide, if you are AWAKE.

How do you start your day?

Do you ask for your inner guidance right away as your feet hit the floor?

Are you excited? "Wow, this is a completely brand new day! The Slate is blank. I'm going to embrace the moment and feel the joy of following my Superpower."

Do you wake up with your to-do list, a daily plan and Your Story?

Do you listen to the Deceptive broadcast of lack and limitation, struggle and strife, and feel the effects on your body?

You create each moment. You wake up, you're breathing, you're present, you're AWAKE, and then you choose.

You get to choose to trust and know that everything's going to be provided that you need. You know that you're going to be guided, and you're open to receive.

You are always between your Inner Guidance and the Deceptive broadcast.

Which do you pick in each moment?

Can you get present to that choice in each moment in your body?

Turning the channel is like setting a boundary. Change the station to something more positive, uplifting and inspiring that feels good to you.

The present is all you have. It's a gift. Are you open to receive it?

Do you allow the Deceptive broadcast to hook you into Your Story and continue to live in the past?

Are you carrying around a sack of yesterday's beliefs (the opposite of Santa's gifts) wherever you go?

It's like going across a street. If you are tuned in, you can easily decide the right time to walk across the street without it affecting the peace of the drivers in their cars. If you are listening to the Deceptive broadcast, your agitated state can then affect the drivers of the cars because you become indecisive.

Every thought you think and feel affects all those around you, whether you are aware of this or not. Your reactions and responses are like a pebble in a pond. It's a ripple effect when you aren't present. They expand out and affect others in your family, community and the world.

Do you believe it? Are you aware of it?

Notice the impacts of your reactions or responses on others around you?

Being in the Chrysalis

As I was in the chrysalis, I would go back and forth between these two broadcasts. I trusted, and then I doubted or questioned. I'd either be certain or let a past pattern of helplessness take over. I could switch from being the forever spiritual optimist, believing there was always a way for everything to work out, to the victim in my relationships or resigned that I would always have health issues.

In Canada, like many western countries, we have socialized medicine. I believe that's our birthright. Part of My Story is that "I believe we need to take care of each other."

However, I stayed away from using the allopathic/traditional Medical system with my daughters, because I had been on pharmaceutical drugs earlier in my life, and realized that wasn't the answer for me after ten years of daily medication.

I had learned through my personal experience that the medical community was doing their best with what they knew, but there was much more that they didn't know about the long term effects on my mental, emotional, and physical well being.

I experienced how similarities of patients were grouped together to build the dis-ease profile, and there was never a concrete answer, except that I was told I had an incurable dis-order.

Thankfully I trusted my inner guidance, and began a journey of mind/body medicine in 1991 which was the last time I took pharmaceutical drugs.

Moving from my own health, to trusting my intuition for my children was very difficult as almost everything in the world pointed to immunization as the answer.

I was in between the two broadcasts.

My Original Story that I had grown up with and believed that "Doctors know best, and immunizations are necessary to help everyone."

Two weeks before my first child was born, I was guided to the book, *What Every Parent Should Know About Childhood Immunization*. By the title, I thought it would be a book to support My Original Story. I was surprised to discover that vaccines were made with aluminum, thimerosal and formaldehyde. I still remember the churning in my stomach as I was reading that information. I was planning on breastfeeding and giving my newborn no sugar, no meat or dairy for the first two years of her life based on what I learned to keep my baby's immune system strong. How could it be wise to give my child aluminium, thimerosal, and formaldehyde? It seemed a lot worse than sugar, meat or dairy.

Here is where My Original Story started to affect me. The doctor told me at our 5 day old check up to bring her back in two months for her first vaccine. I politely told him I was evaluating options at the moment.

He then activated the Deceptive Broadcast using Fear and Guilt. He told me that if I didn't vaccinate her, she wouldn't be allowed in school. As a brand new mother with a 5 day old, I was now being projected into the future 5 years, and out of the NOW.

I felt guided to delay the two month vaccination, did my research, delayed more, met others who had never vaccinated, listened to the calmness that I was feeling about trusting my intuition. The Deceptive Broadcast, and the one I was used to hearing most of my life was saying things like, "You were vaccinated, and you are ok. It's better to trust the doctor than your feelings. She could die if you don't vaccinate her."

I received some new thoughts, "What if our society has traded off building our immune system through childhood dis-eases, creating a society burdened with chronic autoimmune dis-eases reliant on the pharmaceutical industry?"

Hearing Viera Scheibner speak, and reading her book *Vaccination: 100 Years of Orthodox Research* gave me plenty of evidence for not vaccinating, but I still kept hearing the Deceptive broadcast, "What if you are wrong?" "You will be a terrible mom." "Maybe it's best just to do the same as you were raised."

The Deceptive broadcast is always about the future or the past, and never about the NOW. It is tempting and suggestive, where Source / consciousness is a simple prompt. I had to rely on what I was feeling led/prompted to do. It might have been normal to be vaccinated, but there was an angst in my body at the thought of having her immunized that felt abnormal.

I chose what felt natural in my body over what was normal by other's standards. I kept holding off, and eventually my daughters did go to school without any immunizations. I was at peace and had more faith in my guidance each day. My New Story became, "it was my job to keep their immune systems strong so they would stay healthy."

I took them to cranial sacral therapists, chiropractors, naturopaths, acupuncturists, chinese medicine practitioners, and massage therapists. They were treated with homeopathy, aromatherapy, therapeutic touch, Reiki, Body Matrix Repatterning. herbs, organic food, positive language, art, music, etc. All of these alternative or complementary products and treatments were to be proactive in keeping their immune system healthy, as that was part of My New Story.

One day I received another new thought, "Why are those of us, who are being extra responsible for our health paying for alternative therapies? If we were going to the doctor and using pharmaceutical drugs we would get them for free?" "This doesn't quite make sense. Health should be a Natural thing." After all when we cut ourselves, we expect the cut to heal. When we break a bone, we expect the bone to heal with the help of a doctor to reset the fracture. Our body is designed to fix itself naturally.

Wouldn't it make sense that our body is designed to keep us in good health? Isn't it possible that what we consider sickness is actually the body's way of ridding itself of the toxicity, and bringing the body back into balance?

I started to receive thoughts like these:

Our nose runs, because it wants to release.

We cough because we want to expel something out of our body.

We burp or fart to release gas.

We cry to release grief.

We yell to release frustration.

What if health is our birthright?

What if we have been listening to the Deceptive broadcast all this time?

I started to use my own intuition more and more. I followed the guidance given to me about our health and well being. I also had a huge book on alternative treatments, that I referred to if I was questioning an issue. I was open to the idea that **Health was Natural.**

My Superpower led me to Dr. Christiane Northrup, who was a member of the Medical Scientific group of the Circle of Friends. She shared the words of Bruno, "God sends you healing streams, and you need to absorb them daily, because your body is like a battery and it will wear down. You don't have to believe a word I say, but you have a duty to convince yourself."

That was the answer for me with respect to the thought, "Health is our birthright."

This concept from Bruno, that I could open up, Tune-In, and recharge myself to stay healthy was a game changer. I was skeptical, but I liked the idea that I got to decide based on my experience.

If I was approached about this when I was back in the Caterpillar World, I would have rejected it and made fun of it. In fact, I actually did that when in 1989 I was first shown Louise Hay's *You Can Heal Your Life* Book which correlated thoughts with dis-ease. I dismissed it and tossed the book back at the person who showed me.

I understand if you feel this way, because I too, was there once also. I'm glad I stepped into the **"I don't know what I don't know"** part of the Universe. It led me into the Chrysalis of Transformation and to Healing from the Inside Out.

The more I opened up to this idea of aligning myself authentically with this vibration, it was "Wow!" Something so easy and so profound at the same time. Things started shifting!

I have completely convinced myself that Health is Natural. It's a state of being that comes from within. Health is true Wealth. I'll share more about a key healing experience for me, tomorrow, on Day 7 that happened 11/11/11.

I've seen others heal too. I have also heard many medical doctors verify the healings of a variety of "incurable" dis-eases. There is no medical explanation of how it happened except that the person started to absorb the healing streams.

When you completely believe, it's actually a deep inner knowing in your being. A foundational shift through your core. You feel completely different as if every cell in your body has been rejuvenated, recalibrated and reenergized to the latest health software update.

You realize that you can have a world that really does make you light up on all levels. It is like you are a child again, but it happens at whatever age you are now.

I am 57. I'm more excited and at peace about LIFE than ever before. I have the eyes of a child again, and the awe. If you remember that's what I desired when I returned from Africa. I have this new sense of wisdom and humility. I had to die to my ego, in order to be in my best whole new world of joy, health, love, peace, and wealth.

You Have the Power to Choose

You always have a choice in every moment. You are capable of choosing between two ice cream flavours, or which drink you would like or having a bath or a shower, right?

If you can choose everyday things in your life, you can choose to trust what you are being guided to say or do. This is REAL LIFE! The journey to your heart's desires.

You may be like The *Little Engine That Could*, "I think I can. I think I can. I think I can. I think I can." You will get results, but they are within a limited box of your ideas. When you trust your Superpower, you are guided to any of the infinite possibilities that exist outside of the box.

When you let go of control, and trust your intuition, you will be led through the Chrysalis of transformation towards your heart's desires. As you trust, you receive even greater blessings beyond your imagination as that's all that exists in the Best Whole New World. There is much more detail about the benefits of letting go on Day 8.

Which broadcast do you listen to the most today?

Do you notice:

How does it affect your body?

The impacts on others?

The feelings you are left with from listening to it?

Are you ready to turn up the volume on your Superpower

NOW?

If you just read the Tune-In at the beginning of this chapter, and still haven't tuned in yet…do it now.

Tune-In: Palms up, Body open, Happy thought

I'm asking for my inner guidance,

To clearly communicate with me,

In each and every moment,

For my highest and best good.

I'm asking to be open to receive,

This clear communication,

In each and every moment,

For my highest and best good.

And take joyful action on it.

Thank you!

Stay with the feeling in your body for as long as you can. Notice what you are experiencing. Are your palms warm? Are you feeling cold? Do you have tingles? Are you feeling at peace? Do you feel pain anywhere? If so, speak it out. Release it. When you're done receiving, take your hands to your heart, as if you are closing the drawbridge to your castle. You are fully charged, protected, and ready for your day.

Tune-In with ME

https://youtu.be/LNazErJFVgs

There is a great gift in listening or reading as others share in the private Facebook group. Everyone explains how this experience occurs for them a little differently. You may also enjoy contributing to others by commenting on their shares.

Step 3: Watch and/or Listen to Awaken an Aha in You

Kat from Ireland

Tulasi from England

DAY 7 OF 10 - FULLY CHARGED

Did you do the Tune-In yet?

If not, let's do it. Only carry on reading after you have finished receiving the energy and being present to the words.

Step 1: Tune-In. Palms up, Body open, Happy thought

Say out loud:

I'm asking for my inner guidance,

To clearly communicate with me,

In each and every moment,

For my highest and best good.

I'm asking to be open to receive

This clear communication,

In each and every moment,

For my highest and best good.

And to take joyful action on it.

Thank you!

The link below lets you do the energetic Tune-In with me.

https://youtu.be/LNazErJFVgs

When you have finished being present to the words you spoke, and receiving the energetic Tune-In, continue reading.

Do you feel the difference in opening and taking a minute or two

just to get present to your inner guidance?

This is the communication that's being sent to you today, and is being received by you.

Throughout your day, all kinds of messages are being received by you. Some of them you're aware that you're receiving, and some of them you're unaware that you're receiving,

Are you aware of what you're noticing?

The gift is to realize what you experience within yourself.

When you are convinced of how reliable your inner guidance is, everything changes beyond your comprehension, and you really can have your Best Whole New World!

Fully Charged

Today is noticing how you manage your inner guidance.

This will depend on how fully charged you are at any moment.

When your cell phone is hundred percent charged, you know you can carry on long conversations. You can do a Facebook live. You can record a video. You have all kinds of talking and text time. You can watch Youtube or listen to podcasts for long durations.

Contrast that with your cell phone operating at 10 percent. It's going down. You go to record a small video, sometimes it just won't load. Sometimes you are talking, and the call just ends without notice because you've used up all the battery power. There is no more power, and you need to get your phone recharged.

This can happen with your laptop too. We all know the battery depletes and we may need to charge it again to get it through the day. If we are away from an electrical source we have an issue. No charge. No connection. No reception. No communication.

Consider that your body is like a battery. It needs to be charged just like your cell phone and your laptop. It is worn down by all these frequencies around you, like other's opinions, feelings, and the general expression of the world around you.

You're receiving all the time.

If you're receiving positive and inspirational messages or connecting with others in good vibes, this can keep your charge up. Being in nature, listening to or playing music, dancing, meditating, creating and being authentically present to the magnificence around you keeps you operating at a decent charge.

My experience is doing the Tune-In, einstellen or gazing with Braco is how I keep me operating at a full charge.

Step 2: Grab your notebook or Notes, and write the answers

Take a few minutes to get present to how you start your day and how much attention you truly give yourself and your body throughout the day.

Do you:

Get up in the morning and do your Tune-In?

Take the same time for yourself to connect with Source /consciousness that you do for having a shower, getting ready for the day and eating?

Run out the door feeling like you are going to be late?

Wake up on the "wrong side of the bed?"

Respond or react in situations that trigger you or are

unexpected?

Notice how the start of your morning affects you throughout your day.

The experience I had on 11/11/11 taught me how important it is to be fully charged at all times. It was a major exam for me in trusting my inner guidance, without consciously knowing it was coming. Since I was fully charged I passed the exam. I was at that point in my journey, and this is my experience only.

It was a beautiful, extraordinary day on the morning of November 11th in the Greater Toronto Area. I was taking my black Labrador, Shadow, out for a run. I was riding my bicycle, and he was running beside me as I was holding the leash. It was always fun, easy to do, and great exercise for both of us as we went through the neighbourhood.

It was about 7:30 am, as we were rounding the bend for the last hundred meters, and there was a woman with her little dog. Shadow never was distracted, until that day.

He dashed in front of my bike with me holding the leash. I was yanked forward, and my skull crashed onto the pavement as I was without a bike helmet. Thankfully, I was so full of power due to the weekend conference, and the two introductions to the healing streams that week.

As my head hit the pavement, I immediately said to myself, "I do not accept this. I do not accept this." Since we all receive frequencies from others, I kept my head down and never made eye contact with the woman. I wanted to ensure that I was not absorbing her reaction and her concern of what happened to me.

It seemed like time stopped. I grabbed my dog, my bike, and I managed to make it back home in a moment. When I walked into my house, I avoided looking at myself in the foyer's mirrored closet doors. I wanted to ensure I did not take in the idea of what happened.

I grabbed a picture of Bruno Groening, and held that on my forehead. I realized that I had this huge, three-inch bulging contusion on my head. I was immediately in between the two broadcasts.

One was broadcasting from within, "Okay, I can deal with this. I believe anything can be healed. This can too." Remember, Bruno said, "God is the greatest physician. Trust and Believe. Nothing is Impossible for God. Illness doesn't belong to man. Spirit rules Matter."

At the same time, the Deceptive broadcast I was receiving was, "Wow. Oh my gosh. This is big!"

That oh-my-gosh opened the door for all these other thoughts that kept flooding in.

One of those was the story about Liam Neeson's wife, Natasha. She had been skiing, fallen, hit her head, and had thought nothing of it. Three hours later, she was dead.

The Deceptive broadcast was sending thoughts like, "Do you remember those billboards all around the Toronto area?" There were big billboards all over the city. Each displayed a bicycle and a watermelon split open as it impacted the ground. The message was "Wear a helmet. Your head is like a watermelon."

All these thoughts were being received. I started to feel the fear, "Oh my gosh. This is a head injury. I must get myself to the hospital."

The other stream of thoughts that I was receiving were calming instead of alarming.

"Everything is going to be fine. This is your moment to choose what you really believe and take the necessary actions.

I went to my oldest daughter's bedroom. She had been at the Circle of Friends Conference with me, so I felt she would be fully charged. She magically woke up about 30 seconds before I walked into her room, which was unusual.

She just woke up and said, "Hello, mom. You have some regulugen." This is a German word, meaning your body is regulating. She grabbed a bandana, and tied it around my head to hold the photo in place.

Her calmness helped me stay in connection with the calm stream of thoughts.

I then started downstairs to go cook breakfast for my dear friends, Karin and Sylke, that arrived last night. When they walked into the kitchen, they looked at me, and said, "Dear Mrs. Best. We need to do einstellen (which means Tune-In to the healing streams) together." We opened up and tuned in, and asked for help for my health and well being.

In the moment, with the three of us there, I felt an intense stream of energy penetrating my forehead, that I likened to a laser beam. It was very painful. It brought me to tears for about 30 seconds. It was a big release.

Then it was just peaceful. I felt calm and received, "Everything is going to be totally and completely fine."

By the afternoon, my swelling in my forehead was gone. However, I could still feel how spongy my skull was when I touched it.

When my former husband saw me, he was fearful and said, "You need to get yourself to the hospital!" I said, "No, I'm going to be fine." However, I could feel the intensity of his fear, and how it was weakening my conviction in my inner peace. Thankfully my friend, Karin, turned to him and said, "A foot is no different than a head to God." You see, he had a healing of ankle tendinitis the first time he absorbed the healing streams.

The importance of having somebody with more conviction or more experience than I, was crucial in that moment. Her confidence in the healing vibe overcame the fear vibe from him.

My former husband was scared, and kept projecting his concern onto me throughout the day. At one point I almost decided to go to the hospital to make him feel better. It was my eldest daughter who said, "Don't go to the hospital to make him feel better. You're the one that will hear what the doctors are going to say."

I knew she was right. I was the one that was going to have to sit there, and listen to the doctor say, "Your skull is soft," or "We've taken an x-ray, or MRI, and this is what we've seen. There is internal bleeding there." Whatever the doctors would say or do, I had to ask myself am I strong enough to resist their expert advice? My answer was, "No. I would cave in my beliefs with all their knowledge and evidence."

This is why I say it's important to be fully charged each day. When you're fully charged up with energy, you can handle whatever circumstances are presented to you in life. You can follow your inner guidance. You have enough power to do so.

When you're operating at less than full power, you can be susceptible to these other energies that I started to hear, receive, and feel.

Does that make sense?

I knew this was my moment to choose to trust what I believed to be true. I was being responsible to me for what I felt I was being guided to do.

It took a week for all the bruising and discoloration to disappear from my face. The softness in my skull was still present for about six weeks. It became rock hard, after I did an online gazing with Braco. In that five minute gaze, I could feel my skull hardening. It was amazing! I kept knocking on my head to prove that it was hard again. Truly remarkable!

This was the greatest experience and gift to myself ever! I had the confidence to trust that everything was prepared for me to move forward. I had people there that could support me in what I believed. I put my faith in the Source / consciousness that created me, as I was guided to do.

Being fully charged gave me the strength to turn up the volume on my inner guidance, and stay present to the moment.

That day I started to receive new thoughts.

"I use a lot of energy to defend myself against my former husband's fears, judgements, and doubts."

"Imagine how much more energy I would have for others, if I was surrounded by those who were on the same wavelength."

The day 11/11/11 was a new beginning for me as I experienced the radical shift in my physical body from tuning in with my friends. This was a completely transformative moment. I had felt health was natural and my birthright. Now I knew that Spirit ruled Matter. I had convinced myself that Source / consciousness was the greatest physician. No one could tell me otherwise.

Every moment, you have that ability to stay present, and choose what you're feeling led to do. The power is within you always.

The question is how much power do you have at this moment?

Are you feeling the calm presence in your body?

Are you being affected by the Deceptive broadcast?

How loud is your Superpower's volume within you?

Can you easily change the channel?

Do you need to spend more time doing a Tune-In?

Your inner guidance is designed to keep you plugged in so you can thrive freely in joy, health, peace, love, and wealth.

When you stay fully charged and tuned in, you will discover magic happens.

I was able to discern fairly easily between the two broadcasts and know what the Source / consciousness guidance was for me. I had the support around me to keep me connected to my inner guidance.

Who do you surround yourself with regularly?

Do they support you and give you greater confidence in your inner guidance?

Do they share their doubts, opinions and fears with you about

your choices?

Consider that you are absorbing others' support or doubt like a sponge. Your reception of your inner guidance is being impacted. It is similar to your cell phone only having a 20 - 30 % charge left. You start to focus that your phone charge is going down, and it is distracting. Similarly, you could focus more on what's not working versus working.

How charged or tune up you are, dictates how and what you're able to discern in a moment.

Are you listening to your Inner Guidance or the Deceptive broadcast?

You are being hit by tons of text messages, Instagram notifications, Facebook messages communicating good, bad or indifferent information. You could be listening or hearing about the latest news or it could just be playing in the background.

In Canada, the news plays in hospitals, in elevators, in restaurants etc. It's always in the background. When I ask about it, the answer usually is, "I don't notice it anymore." or "I just stop listening to it." They are still being affected by it, and they have stopped noticing how it affects them.

You may notice your positivity declines a little. You may start to identify with that frequency. You may or may not notice how it affects you.

You might pick up on the frequency of suffering or confusion. It starts to seep in. Your conversation or thoughts shift. You identify and empathize with them, and you take in some of their lower frequency. This diminishes your battery supply. You need to be recharged again. If you ignore these moments, your energy drains further. You become more open and susceptible to the multiple other frequencies out there from the Deceptive broadcast.

Stop in those moments, and do the Tune-In. Find a joyous thought and connect to it. Tune-In with me. I'll watch a Bruno or Braco YouTube video if I need an extra charge. Make yourself a priority to feel the peace.

In this hypnotic trance the world has been under, we have categorized many things as stress and we have made that normal. Stress may be considered normal. **Stress is not natural.**

When I was in my twenties, climbing the corporate ladder, people would say, "You're so successful and everything's going great in your life." I completely fit in with what was expected of me. However, my body told another story. I had dis-ease. I had dis-order. The massage therapist, (yes, I went 30 years ago) would say, "You have stress knots, the size of golf balls all over your back."

Now, today 30 years later, the stress that had manifested into golf balls is gone. I'm loose, I am healthy. I know how to let go. I'm naturally in alignment with the vibration that gives me presence and presents me with this body.

Notice your Energy Levels in Different Situations.

Notice what your body is saying to you.

Is it saying I need food, a nap, a walk, or is it saying I need to be reenergized?

Do you:

Say, "I can't do it right now. I have more important things to do?"

Notice that you reacted because your charge was low?

Allow yourself time to Tune-In and recharge?

Open up, hands up, palms up, ready to receive?

Ask for the divine connection to be fully recharged and rebooted?

I tested and retested my inner guidance, until I convinced myself that I had an amazing Superpower that was always producing great results. I also realized that hanging around with others, that questioned my intuition, depleted my energy resources.

These simple little phrases have transformed my life. "I'm asking for the Source connection. I'm asking for help. I need guidance on what my next step is to be."

I've discovered that keeping it simple is so much easier.

I have experienced the healing energy when I have tuned in, and the positive effects on my body, mind and soul. I want you to experience what your Superpower feels like in your body too!

When you are fully charged, you have the power to transform in every moment.

Recognize your power levels as you go through the day.

Are you starting to become aware of when you're more susceptible to other frequencies?

Have you noticed that simply opening up and asking for your

inner guidance has had a benefit in how you handled your experiences?

Are you noticing what's working?

Have you consciously noticed that your Superpower delivers benefits?

Each day that you Tune-In and recharge, you are enhancing your ability to receive the good vibes. You are able to discern between the two broadcasts, and to see how Your Story acts as a filter for your inner guidance. Your Superpower is getting stronger!

If you just read the Tune-In at the beginning of this chapter, and still haven't tuned in yet…do it now.

Tune-In: Palms up, Body open, Happy thought

I'm asking for my inner guidance,

To clearly communicate with me,

In each and every moment,

For my highest and best good.

I'm asking to be open to receive,

This clear communication,

In each and every moment,

For my highest and best good.

And take joyful action on it.

Thank you!

Stay with the feeling in your body for as long as you can. Notice what you are experiencing. Are your palms warm? Are you feeling cold? Do you have tingles? Are you feeling at peace? Do you feel pain anywhere? If so, speak it out. Release it. When you're done receiving, take your hands to your heart, as if you are closing the drawbridge to your castle. You are fully charged, protected, and ready for your day.

Tune-In with ME

https://youtu.be/LNazErJFVgs

Sharing in the private Facebook group what you notice today about how charged you are, and what you notice that you are noticing, will be helpful. Everybody explains how this experience is occurring for them a little differently.

Step 3: Watch and/or Listen to Awaken an Aha in You

Deb from Australia

Kat from Ireland

DAY 8 OF 10 - LET IT GO

Did you do the Tune-In yet?

If not, let's do it. Only carry on reading after you have finished receiving the energy and being present to the words.

Step 1: Tune-In. Palms up, Body open, Happy thought

Say out loud:

I'm asking for my inner guidance,

To clearly communicate with me,

In each and every moment,

For my highest and best good.

I'm asking to be open to receive

This clear communication,

In each and every moment,

For my highest and best good.

And to take joyful action on it.

Thank you!

The link below lets you do the energetic Tune-In with me.

https://youtu.be/LNazErJFVgs

When you have finished being present to the words you spoke, and receiving the energetic Tune-In, continue reading.

Do you feel the difference in opening and taking a minute or two just to get present to your inner guidance?

We are almost done with Trusting Your Intuition - Discover Your Superpower in 10 days. .

Are you noticing that you have gained confidence in trusting your inner guidance?

Are you doing the Tune-In daily, and noticing the effect on your body?

Most feel a difference in their body when they do the Tune-In with me, as opposed to doing it on their own. Take advantage of doing it with me. I have listened to my own Tune-Ins when I'm feeling thwarted, and immediately I'm present again.

Step 2: Grab your notebook or open Notes, and answer the questions

First, open your hands and ask your inner guidance to give you the answer. Here's the question:

What do you need to let go of today?

What is stopping you from trusting your inner guidance all the time?

When you're listening, are you discovering that your inner guidance is clearly communicating to you each day, in each moment?

Are you more aware of the sensations in your body?

Did you get a sensation in your body as you were reading the above sentence?

Was it an exciting sensation, a dreading one, or something completely different?

Most people have found it difficult to let something go in case they might need it in the future. Basically, they operate from a place of lack. What they are really saying by holding on to something is, "If I need it in the future, there's no other way I can receive this." Does this make sense?

It is uncomfortable for them to be in the gap - the space between letting it go and what is in the future. This is the opposite of trusting your inner guidance.

When you trust, you let go and are in the space of the unknown to you, but your inner guidance knows, as it's connected to Source / consciousness. Practising this with "stuff" leads you to be able to live moment by moment, as you learn that LIFE is in the present, not the past nor the future. LIFE is the experience of the NOW.

Let it Go

What do you need to let go of now?

The thought that came to you could be a simple thought like, "Remember that shirt in your closet that you wanted to get rid of? Give it away today." Or it could say, "Go and clean out a drawer." It could be, "Let that relationship go." "Time for a new car."

You could have received the thought to release resistance or procrastination or your story about your beliefs.

The key here is to follow the thought as it's your experience.

What does your body feel like when you read these statements?

What health belief do you need to let go of now?

Could it be a belief like, "I inherited it." "The doctor told me.....
There's nothing I can do." "I have this ..... Dis-ease." "I need to
take this ...... to help my ......dis-order."

What part of Your Story do you need to let go of now?

This could be related to your job, money or relationship. "Once I
have attained this" or "when this happens...... I'll make the move."

Can you let go of the idea that you need to hold on to anything?

What if a perceived tragedy struck, and your house was wiped out,
could you trust the Universe to provide what you need?

Can you let go of the idea that you have to DO something instead
of TRUSTING your inner guidance moment by moment?

Take time to be with these questions.

If you have a dis-ease, dis-order, pain, or stress, are you willing
to let them go?

Do you believe it could be that easy?

If the answer is, "No", then write out all the reasons why you are
100% sure you CAN'T let go of The Story you've been told or
read regarding your situation.

As you are writing notice:

What is your body feeling?

What thoughts are you receiving?

Do you want to distract yourself?

What are you noticing about this process of letting go?

Then allow yourself to get up and shake it off, or listen to this song,

"Let it Go" from the movie Frozen.

https://youtu.be/ImKzSpGXqOE

The concept of letting go, to allow more flow, was first introduced to me while I was studying to become a certified Feng Shui consultant about 25 years ago.

During that year, we visited a house every other week. It was amazing to see the presence of the homeowner's issue in their material stuff.

Here are three examples:

The owner had all her broken things stored in her inner child and creativity part of her house. This symbolized the unresolved issues she had with her children.

The woman, who wanted to have a successful business on her own, was surrounded and overwhelmed by her husband's stuff which was overpowering her and her self expression.

The man had his whole basement packed with stuff that might help someone one day, but he could barely move to get in, and he had physical dis-ease for over 20 years.

I've been in lots of houses over these few decades. I've seen the impact of adding cures in the house and to shift the placement of furniture. The fastest shift in energy I've seen is clearing a closet, cupboards, a corner of a room, or moving the sofa to get rid of the dust bunnies. It's like seeing the old energy leaving the building.

Letting go allows for new to arrive.

If you keep listening to the same Deceptive Broadcast, and keep replaying Your Story, and never turn the channel, then your home most definitely reflects your way of being.

Every placement of every object in your house is an energetic representation of what's going on in and around you. It's your box that you are comfortable with right now.

Your inner guidance knows how to get you out of the box. You have to turn up the volume on your Superpower. It's through your experience that this happens.

Children are Great Teachers

When my children were young, they were such a great blessing teaching me about letting go.

I was schooled through the experience of watching them.

I had created a giveaway drawer. The rule was something had to go before something else came in the house. I noticed that at a young age, under seven, they already knew what they didn't want and would put it in the give away drawer.

Sometimes they would take the gift that Grandma and Grandpa had recently given them and immediately stick it in the drawer. I would pull it out, because I listened to the thoughts that said, "It cost hundreds of dollars," or "What do they know at four years of age," or "I'm sure they will want it eventually."

I would take the chemistry set or the lovely piece of clothing that they bought and stash it aside, thinking next year they would want it.

I learned that when they decided that they didn't want it, they didn't want it. It was never used. I even moved houses with some of those things like the chemistry set. I remember believing the thought,

"One day they're going to want to use the chemistry set." Nope. I was wrong.

They were clear from the first moment at a young age. They didn't want it. They let it go

They would naturally go through stages of mess and cleanliness in their rooms. It was so synergistic. They would clean up their room, give away a bunch of stuff, and more would arrive in an unexpected way almost immediately.

There would be the knock or ring at the door. Surprise, there's this box of stuff at the door for them.

I was doing some work with a client. I was helping her demolish her debts. She worked for Nickelodeon in New York City. We never had a conversation about my kids, other than I had two daughters.

She decided that she wanted to say thanks and sent a box of stuff for the girls. They were delighted. Some of the gifts they loved, and some of the SpongeBob videos were watched once, if that, and put in the give away drawer immediately.

It's amazing what can happen when you let go. It is quite fun! My family has moved a lot of times, and this was part of my journey to experience the art of letting go. Each time we went through a transition. We would purge most of the things and start all over again. This taught me to trust over and over again. I built my confidence in my inner guidance to let go, and that whatever I needed always showed up in the perfect time.

Trusting the Timing of the Decluttering Experience

I don't know if this happens in your neighbourhood, but in The Greater Toronto area, when people are done with things they put them out by the street for people to pick up and take for free.

One day, I received the thought to clear and reorganize a room. I was left with a bunch of my daughter's creative materials of various sizes. I knew I wanted this behind closed doors versus open shelving.

I had nothing in the house to accomodate my vision. Now everything was in a pile all out on the floor. I did receive a thought like, "Now you've got a mess, because you have nothing to put it in!" I smiled to myself as I knew my Superpower had an answer.

Then I suddenly received the thought, "Take the garbage out now." I usually would do that the next morning. I literally walked out my door and poof! Three doors down, across the street, a neighbour had put this big beautiful Mahogany desk and a Mahogany cabinet out front with a sign "Free."

The wonderful cabinet was absolutely perfect. It was designed for the storage needs perfectly, like I had custom ordered it.

This all happened in about two hours. I received the thought to reorganize. I followed. It appeared that I was left with a mess. I followed my inner guidance to take the garbage out, and then the universe provided the solution.

If I didn't start to clean, reorganize and let go, I wouldn't have been open to receive the perfect solution of the custom cabinet, right?

This is how I have learned that my inner guidance saves me time. I follow it's schedule, since it is connected to everyone and everything. Imagine the time wasted going shopping for a cabinet?!

Ask your inner guidance, what do you need to release and let go of today.

It could be something at work. It could be to let go of a project. Let go of a relationship. It might be a friend that you've been having difficulty with for a long time, always hoping things will change.

Notice what you're noticing.

What does it feel like when you get guided to take action?

Are you feeling, "Yes! I'm going for it?"

And noticing your body feels joyful with the new possibility after taking action? Or, are you suddenly aware that you're listening to the Deceptive broadcast that says, "No. Not now. You have better things to do." Do you notice that you suddenly have all kinds of other things that distract you from your answer?

You could be feeling like I did when my kids went to giveaway stuff. I was resisting, and listening to the channel that said, "No, no, no. That's too valuable. They will need this. They can't do that because it was just given to them." Thoughts kept coming to me, like "You just don't give away gifts that were given to you."

Notice the thoughts that you are receiving.

What you are feeling as you listen?

Notice if you are receiving the thought, "Yes, it would be good to have it gone," but then you start to experience resistance in taking the action to do it. Have the experience without judgement. Let go and follow your inner guidance. The experience is your experience.

I guarantee you there's always more abundance. There's more gifts and blessings than you can ever imagine. It's amazing what goes on when you can truly appreciate that you're being cleared out. Think of how beautiful a butterfly is and the freedom it has compared to a caterpillar. There's so much more that "you don't know, that you don't know!" Open and Receive the journey to your heart's desires!

Notice if you need to do some physical activity to release all the energy in and around you, as you let go of the material, emotional, mental and spiritual. Let it all go!

If you just read the tune in at the beginning of this chapter, and still haven't tuned in yet...do it now.

Tune-In: Palms up, Body open, Happy thought

I'm asking for my inner guidance,

To clearly communicate with me,

In each and every moment,

For my highest and best good.

I'm asking to be open to receive,

This clear communication,

In each and every moment,

For my highest and best good.

And take joyful action on it.

Thank you!

Stay with the feeling in your body for as long as you can. Notice what you are experiencing. Are your palms warm? Are you feeling cold? Do you have tingles? Are you feeling at peace? Do you feel pain anywhere? If so, speak it out. Release it. When you're done receiving, take your hands to your heart, as if you are closing the drawbridge to your castle. You are fully charged, protected, and ready for your day.

Tune-In with ME

https://youtu.be/LNazErJFVgs

There have been some impactful shares in the private Facebook group. Some shared that they noticed that they were guided to do things over these seven days, but they actually ignored the thought that they received.

Later they realized, after the initial prompting was rejected, that their guidance was preparing them for what was ahead. If they had followed the guidance, they would've been prepared for the change in plans.

These are fabulous realizations, and this is how each of us learns. This is all part of your journey to become aware of your inner guidance, your Superpower, and to trust it confidently!

It does help you and others, whether you know it or not. People listen and read, but may refrain from commenting. Know that you are impacting others! We are all in this together co creating our experiences.

You could share: What are you going to release? What showed up for you when you were guided to let go of it? What choices did you make? What experiences did you have? I look forward to hearing or reading!

Step 3: Watch and/or Listen to Awaken an Aha in You

Annelle from Poland

Christine from Ireland

DAY 9 OF 10 - COMMITTED & UNATTACHED

Did you do the Tune-In yet?

If not, let's do it. Only carry on reading after you have finished receiving the energy and being present to the words.

Step 1: Tune-In. Palms up, Body open, Happy thought

Say out loud:

I'm asking for my inner guidance

To clearly communicate with me,

In each and every moment,

For my highest and best good.

I'm asking to be open to receive

This clear communication,

In each and every moment,

For my highest and best good.

And to take joyful action on it.

Thank you!

The link below lets you do the energetic Tune-In with me.

https://youtu.be/LNazErJFVgs

When you have finished being present to the words you spoke, and receiving the energetic Tune-In, continue reading.

Do you feel the difference in opening and taking a minute or two just to get present to your inner guidance?

This could be Day 9 or Chapter 9 depending on how quickly you have been reading the book. Either way is fine. **The important part of the journey is to have your experiences and become more aware of what's really going on in you instead of what's outside of yourself.**

Changing your focus to your body and what messages you are receiving, can be very empowering. It's an important realization when you discover how much is actually going on in your mind and body that you have been ignoring or are just oblivious to each day.

Doing the simple quick inner guidance energetic Tune-In recharges your inner guidance system so you are able to be more present to the thoughts you receive and the impacts on your body.

After all, what does it matter what anyone else is saying or doing, or what's happening in the universe or anywhere on the planet, if you are completely numb to the impacts on your body?

This 10 day experience is giving you simple and effective tools to keep developing your Superpower.

As you focus on yourself, you become more aware of what's happening to your body as you interact with the world around you. There is a realization that you have freedom to choose to respond versus react to situations outside of your control. .

You can choose:

To accept a message or delete it.

To turn the channel or keep listening to the message.

To turn off the Deceptive broadcast or to turn it up.

You can even decide to do something that gives you joy!

It can be an abrupt awakening for some, that each person is responsible for what they are listening to and the effects on their body. You may be used to blaming others for the effects on your life. There is a payoff when you can point a finger at someone else, because you never have to change or accept that change can happen in your favour.

When you realize that you have the freedom to choose to respond, there is a new level of control within yourself. You begin to trust you are in the right place at the right time.

This recognition of your Superpower, gives birth to a whole new freedom and way of being as you realize that you can rely on Trusting your Intuition/Inner Guidance.

You may need more experiences on a certain day to convince yourself before moving on to the next step. It's all good!

Maybe you stopped reading the book, and have just picked it up again. You may have experienced some resistance and needed to have your own unique experience with the Universe before continuing. It's all good!

Trusting your inner guidance takes practice. Practice breeds confidence. One day you'll realize that you only ever have one choice and that's to follow IT. The volume of your Superpower is so loud that's all you are ever tuned in to at any given moment.

Then you can move on, living in Surrender - the Ultimate Trust. Being in joy, health, peace, love and wealth, and having the freedom to be present to each moment as you are on a journey of your heart's desires.

Committed and Unattached

Are you ready? A new level of freedom in trusting and believing awaits you.

Most people never get to experience this as they like to control or like to have the illusion of control.

It doesn't matter what you've been working on manifesting. If it is not in alignment with your highest and best good, then your inner guidance will guide you in a new direction.

It's important to have put aside what you think you know about the Universe, as you need to be able to discern clearly at this point what is REALLY happening in and around you.

Using my 11/11/11 cycling accident as an example, I was committed to stepping into continuous new levels of awareness. I was stunned to have my skull crush into the pavement to make this happen. I would have preferred a different experience. When it did, I had to surrender. I had to be completely unattached to the process, and follow step by step. To trust and believe that I was being guided. I could count on this fact.

It is in the moment, when you are given a situation that is completely surprising, that your commitment to your inner guidance is tested.

Step 2: Grab your notebook or open Notes, and answer the questions

Does a situation come to mind, for yourself, that tested your faith or inner guidance previously?

Are you able to see it differently now?

Was the Deceptive broadcast running interference in the situation?

Can you identify the helping forces that were giving you the strength to trust and believe that all will be ok?

It is such a fabulous time when you have these experiences, because you realize that your Superpower shifts your perceived reality from Your Story to keeping you present in the moment. The gift of NOW.

Did you Let "it" Go?

In the last chapter, or yesterday, we talked about letting go. You asked your inner guidance, "What do I need to let go of today?"

Someone in the private Facebook group said they had to let go of "expectations." Everybody has something to let go of all the time. The truth is you are designed to LET GO. You breathe in oxygen, and let go carbon dioxide. **You are committed to breathing, but unattached as to how the oxygen shows up, right?**

The more honest you are with yourself about what you can and are willing to let go of right now, the faster your ability to receive.

This is an important one as the volume becomes louder on your Superpower. It becomes so clear, it's the only broadcast that you hear.

It is like the door gets smaller and smaller for you to go through, as you can only bring your authentic self with zero belongings. It could also be that you are becoming lighter as you have let go of all the dense energy from the Deceptive broadcast.

There is also this idea that you are ascending to a higher vibration. You're being calibrated to a higher frequency, like a high pitched C, or in perfect pitch.

You are committed to your inner guidance. You are also unattached to how you are guided, because you always trust the process.

Unattached is the experience, the journey, is how your heart's desires show up. It is moment by moment. One experience, and another experience. It is being present to what is actually happening on all levels at that moment.

Being committed and unattached is following and going with the flow. Trusting and believing. You know that even if the goals that you set aren't being met, it's all perfectly fine. Everything is happening for everyone in perfect order.

If you are attached to the results, you could be wanting to control the outcome. Hence, you experience more stress when things aren't going as planned or the way you anticipated or desired. You essentially start listening more closely to the Deceptive broadcast.

Are you fairly methodical with your finances? Your income covers your expenses and then you put money towards your savings and investments. You are committed to having healthy finances for retirement. An unexpected situation happens, like the US financial crisis in 2008, where the housing market tanked due to an industry wide mortgage scam. Investments and retirement plans tanked in the market.

If you were attached to your financial situation, you could have had an emotional breakdown. The stress of "Now what?" was huge for many.

If you were unattached, you would know that everything is fine, and that here is another plan for your retirement.

You would be open to receiving the new information.

If you are in business, you could be attached to the results of launching a product or service.

You have a goal for so many people to show up on your webinar. You are doing everything you can, and even using the law of attraction to work for you.

Let's say you have a goal of 100 people showing up to your webinar. You feel that if you hit that goal, then you will feel like it's a success. You are attached. If only 10 people show up, you make it mean that you failed or that you didn't do a good enough job, etc.

Inner guidance is vastly different than the masculine principles of SMART goals. SMART stands for Specific, Measurable, Attainable, Realistic, and Timely.

My experience with inner guidance is that I get a better result than what I imagined, in a way that I never knew existed. Others have had that experience too when they focus on heart's desires vs immediate results.

The Journey of Trusting

A group of German youth, travelled from Bavaria to Hamburg, because they felt guided to spread the word on divine healing. They were there all day and one person engaged them in conversation and was very interested.

This one person was a medical student, who had never heard anything like this before. Nothing is incurable? He was told otherwise in his studies. He was intrigued, and wanted to learn more.

This student became a doctor, and was responsible for starting the medical and scientific group of the Circle of Friends which has hundreds of medical practitioners all around the world believing in the teaching that God is the greatest physician.

Was their trip a success? Yes. They followed their inner guidance.

It's never about the numbers or the outcome. It's only a small part of the journey. The experience is the gift.

Your inner guidance is always going to guide you. You can allow yourself to enjoy your journey or you can delude yourself that you are in control. It takes practice, as most of us have expectations of how something is going to turn out. We want a plan or a guarantee or the idea that this is going to work out.

All these ideas are attachments, and stop you from really experiencing your Superpower. You can have moments and realizations that it works for you. True Surrender is a whole new world. Your best whole new world. More than you ever imagined!

You're committed to the journey and unattached to the results.

It's like, you're sauntering along on the path and you are soaking in the whole experience, on every sensual level. It's just a beautiful day!

Then suddenly you step in a mud puddle. All that happened is that you stepped in a mud puddle. You have to clean off the mud later. Just an experience.

Do you brood about it all day?

Do you feel you have to peel the layers to discover why you stuck your foot in the mud puddle?

We were given this LIFE, to experience IT. If you come across something or encounter an issue, it's just an experience that you are actively engaged in at that moment.

Today, notice what you are noticing about your experience.

Learning to be in the present moment is about becoming aware of your body in that moment, and how it is reacting to the messages that you are receiving from outside yourself.

When you can be completely committed to trusting your inner guidance, your Superpower is so loud, it's the only broadcast you hear. You will discover that your free will and your inner guidance are one.

Yes, there are moments, like mud puddles. You can search for the meaning of why you stepped in the mud puddle or ask about the lesson but the mud puddle is just a mud puddle. It's in those moments you get to discern, to ask for clarity. See what the experience actually is, and what you may still need to release.

Being attached limits your experience. It can create Doubt or Uncertainty.

Many times I have heard, "I don't understand. I was guided to call them. I thought for sure, they were going to buy my product or service, but they didn't. I must have been wrong for thinking that was my inner guidance."

Consider that the gift of the experience was different than your attachment to the sale. There must have been another reason your inner guidance directed you to have that experience.

This is the important part of being fully charged, and being aware in the moment. You are able to discern.

Great things happen when you let go and trust the process.

A lifetime ago, my former husband and I were on a mini getaway. We tuned in when we woke up. We had set an intention for our day. We asked to have fun, laughter and enjoy ourselves today.

As we were driving around enjoying ourselves, we wondered where we should go for lunch? We received two different thoughts. One, we could go grab some groceries, and go have a nice romantic meal back at the resort. Two, we could go to one of our favorite restaurants in a nearby town.

We tuned in to our inner guidance, asked the question, "What was in our highest and best good?"

We both received, "Go to your favorite restaurant." When we arrived, it was closed for the season. I wondered, "Why would we be guided here since it's closed? That doesn't make any sense, because I really liked the idea of a romantic encounter back at the resort."

I was a little miffed, and then we noticed there was a real estate sales office across the street. They were selling new homes around the golf course. We went in to take a look since we were here.

The sales rep started to show us the plan of the new homes division and he was so funny. We were laughing and laughing. It was one of those gut wrenching laughing experiences. Everything he said was so funny. We were laughing and laughing and laughing and laughing.

Then I got it! This was one of the things that we had asked for in the morning when we tuned in. We had asked for laughter, and that's why we were guided to the restaurant.

We thought we were going to the restaurant for lunch, but we were guided there to end up at the Sales Rep office and have that laughter. Our inner guidance knew where we would have laughter, and in the process we learned to let go of the attachment to the answer we received. Do you understand the process?

Day 9 is all about receiving a thought and taking action on it without being attached to the outcome of your inner guidance.

Are you up for it?

Or does the mere thought make you cringe with anxiety or doubt?

Are you resisting the guidance?

Consider it's because you have never been where you want to go, and that's uncomfortable for you. It is referred to as "Getting out of your Comfort Zone." It's the don't know what you know part of the Universe.

Here are three experiences of being committed and unattached to the results

Health Transformation Course

In late 2016 I was guided to join a program that used a facebook group. I met a lot of great people, and one was a woman who had a brain injury for 9 years. I reached out, and told her about the Circle of Friends. She attended a community hour in Portland. It didn't feel right for her. I understood.

As a community leader for the Circle of Friends, I observed some people held on to their ailments instead of letting go. They came to receive the healing streams believing that's all they needed to do to heal. However they never truly gave up their burdens. Most had many layers of beliefs about their dis-ease or dis-order that they held onto like security blankets.

I received the thought to create a Health Transformation program. It would be a combination of letting go of beliefs and absorbing the healing streams. Every day we would tune in together so the participant would connect with my healing vibes. Flora was willing to test it out.

I was committed and unattached. I had 24 hours to receive the topic, create the video, write the text, and record the healing audio Tune-In, as I stayed one day ahead of her. None of it was planned. We did a weekly call to break through any other stuff that came up for her.

The result of me being committed and unattached, is illustrated in her words:

"I am not sure how the transformation really worked, but it was your clarity and love and holding the space and never letting go, even when I did not believe you...I still feel like I want your hand to be available. My transformation from working with you on your Health Transformation course is just too huge to speak clearly about now. I am BACK, but not where I was before. I am full of joy, love, clarity, patience, purpose and this great gift of life like I never experienced it."

Global Party Healing from the Inside Out

Then at the End of May 2017 I was given the idea to interview others about their healings on the June solstice. I had learned about how to do a virtual summit with recordings in both my Mastermind group and from Online Marketing Business School. It seemed doable.

However, I was guided to do something completely different. I was being guided to host a LIVE 30 hour marathon, and call it "Global Party Healing from the Inside Out" We would start each interview with music. There would be dance, and great stories of transformation from around the world.

The vision that I was given to express was: **One billion people being healed from the inside out, trusting their inner guidance, enjoying the journey of their heart's desires, and living in their best whole new world.**

Seemed like a huge number to me, one billion people healed, but being committed and unattached, I spoke it out. Now as the world changes quickly, it seems like anything is possible, and one billion could be a small number!

I followed my guidance every step of the way, as solstice was in less than 30 days. I knew about 3 people that could participate, and had to trust Source / consciousness for the whole experience. One by one I was guided to a person in various parts of the planet, who had experienced some kind of body, mind, and or spirit healing. I interviewed 30 people in 30 hours. All of them LIVE on Facebook. Pure surrender as we had never used the BeLive platform as it just came out of beta testing days before. For some people, it was their very first LIVE. We all had faith, because I had conveyed that Source / consciousness was running the show, so all we could do was TRUST!

Braco's 50th Birthday Party

I was guided to fly to Zagreb for Braco's 50th birthday party in

2017. Yet my daughters and I felt it was the last time we were ever going to see each other. I felt like I might die.

We all felt the raw emotion. Tears and grief flowed out of my body. I went through the process of ensuring all legal matters were in place in case of death. All three of us knew in our bodies that everything was perfect and my trip was the correct choice, but all this emotion was flowing out. I followed my guidance.

Friends couldn't fathom that I was getting on an airplane when I felt like it was the last time I was going to see my daughters, but that's about being committed and unattached. My body was at peace with the guidance, but there was a release going on that I didn't understand. I allowed the tears to flow, and trusted the calm presence inside me. Sharing this experience with others helped them to trust and believe on a whole new level.

Leaving Zagreb, I caught a taxi at 5 am to the airport. The city was sleeping. The gentleman turned off the main road and headed into an industrial area. The Deceptive broadcast started, "OMG this is like the movies, where they take you to an abandoned building and snuff you out! No one knows where you are. You have no cell service. This is what you were fearing."

My body was completely calm, and full of power. I simply asked, "We are going to the airport, right?" He responded, "I'm married." I giggled to myself wondering what that had to do with my question. I replied, "I remember being on the main highway when I arrived." He responded, "We were taking a short cut, because of construction." The Deceptive broadcast kept playing, wanting me to be fearful based on the past. I kept my presence in the NOW of my peaceful body knowing everything was fine. After about 7 minutes, he turned back onto the main road, and said, "See here we are!"

It was a great experience. Life changing actually. Afterwards, I realized it was my mother's spirit leaving us and that was the emotion we were all feeling. Saying a final goodbye as she completed her transition.

Notice today:

Where your inner guidance is guiding you.

If you are attached or unattached to your goals and results.

What are you feeling about the experience?

What comes up for you during the day?

The more clarity you have about what you are actually experiencing, the better.

If you just read the Tune-In at the beginning of this chapter, and still haven't tuned in yet…do it now.

Tune-In: Palms up, Body open, Happy thought

I'm asking for my inner guidance,

To clearly communicate with me,

In each and every moment,

For my highest and best good.

I'm asking to be open to receive,

This clear communication,

In each and every moment,

For my highest and best good.

And take joyful action on it.

Thank you!

Stay with the feeling in your body for as long as you can. Notice what you are experiencing. Are your palms warm? Are you feeling cold? Do you have tingles? Are you feeling at peace? Do you feel pain anywhere? If so, speak it out. Release it. When you're done receiving, take your hands to your heart, as if you are closing the drawbridge to your castle. You are fully charged, protected, and ready for your day.

Tune-In with ME

https://youtu.be/LNazErJFVgs

Step 3: Watch and/or Listen to Awaken an Aha in You

Maria from England

Hope from USA

Day 10 of 10 - I Trust My Superpower

Did you do the Tune-In yet?

If not, let's do it. Only carry on reading after you have finished receiving the energy and being present to the words.

Step 1: Tune-In. Palms up, Body open, Happy thought

Say out loud:

I'm asking for my inner guidance,

To clearly communicate with me,

In each and every moment,

For my highest and best good.

I'm asking to be open to receive,

This clear communication,

In each and every moment,

For my highest and best good.

And to take joyful action on it.

Thank you!

The link below lets you do the energetic Tune-In with me.

https://youtu.be/LNazErJFVgs

When you have finished being present to the words you spoke, and receiving the energetic Tune-In, continue reading.

Do you feel the difference in opening and taking a minute or two

just to get present to your inner guidance?

It's Day 10. Give yourself a round of applause.

Have you been applying what I've shared so you can have your own experience?

If yes, give yourself another round of applause.

If you have just been reading, skipping the Tune-In and digesting this with your ego mind, then give yourself a round of applause.

The seed has been planted. It will grow. One day you will realize how awesome your Superpower is within you.

However this experience has been for you, all is perfect. Trust the Process.

Step 2: Grab your notebook or open Notes, and answer the questions

What's the biggest Aha that you received about your Superpower?

Describe in detail how you operated before, and how you are going to operate now each day.

Do you Trust Your Inner Guidance more now than on Day 1?

On a scale of 1 to 10, where do you rate trusting your inner guidance now?

Did your experience over these 10 days convince you that you have untapped resources in your Superpower?

If you spent the time doing the Tune-In with me then I know you felt sensations in your body that you had probably never felt before. One woman said to me, "I've done all kinds of energy work, but my lip has never tingled and it always tingles when I Tune-In with you." Another reported, "I do the Tune-In every morning, but I love doing it with you as I tingle everywhere."

Keep doing the Tune-In, listening, experiencing it, and recognizing what's going on in your body. It will become easier to let go, and trust the process of being committed and unattached.

Entering the Chrysalis of Transformation can be short or long depending on how charged you are each day and how attached you are to the Caterpillar World. This book is similar to a lighthouse. I've shared my experiences of becoming a butterfly, like sending out the light from the shore to guide you to your Best Whole New World. Your Superpower can get you there on your own, or you can do it with me, one on one or in a group. However you are guided, it is perfect for you.

On Day 1, I asked you to write down what you believed about your inner guidance. This is where the journey began. If you did write it down, then you have something to reference. Is your answer the same?

On Day 2, I asked you what brings your body joy? Have you become more aware when your body is unhappy or stressed, and able to notice this faster. Are you stopping to ask what it is telling you?

On Day 3, you began to recognize that you're receiving thoughts, ideas, and even vibrations that you have previously believed you thought to be in your mind. Are you more comfortable with that idea that you are receiving thoughts and not thinking thoughts? Are you changing the channel more often? Pushing the off button faster?

On Day 4, I asked you to consult your inner guidance during your action packed day. Have you started doing that more now? Are you going with the flow more? Have you noticed that you have less frustration when plans are changed, and you are trusting the timing?

On Day 5, I asked you about Your Story, and to consider how that influences the way that you are listening to your inner guidance. What revelations have you had and continue to have about Your Story?

On Day 6, it was all about the two main broadcasts in the Universe. There's the main Source /consciousness one, connected to your inner guidance, and there's the Deceptive one full of reasons of lack, limitation, justifications, figuring, rationalizations, etc. Are you more aware of which one you are listening to each day? Have you felt how much energy it takes to deal with the Deceptive broadcast?

On Day 7, it was all about noticing how your day goes when you are operating at different charges. Did you feel that you could Tune-In easier to your inner guidance when you are fully charged? When your energy was low, were you susceptible to the Deceptive broadcast?

On Day 8, it was about letting go, and for many this can be a blessing or a burden. Which did you feel? What was your realization about how you perceive letting go and decluttering? Did you trust the Universe to help you to do the decluttering?

On Day 9, it was about being committed and unattached. Going with the flow of your inner guidance. Trusting the process. Taking one step at a time, with a complete knowing that all will be for your highest and best good. It's always for your highest and best good, even though it can seem like you are going in the opposite direction.

Breakdown the Caterpillar leads to Breakthrough the Butterfly.

Step 2: Grab your notebook or open Notes, and answer the questions

Can you say, "I Trust My Superpower"?

How does it feel when you say it aloud? How does it feel when you write it?

Do those words flow easily out of your mouth or on paper?

Notice if your body has any particular sensations that are going on when you speak or write these words, "I Trust My Intuition/Inner Guidance."

Say it or write it slowly being present to each word.

Maybe as you say or write "trust", there starts to be a slight uncomfortable feeling in your stomach or gut. Maybe you have a slight sensation when you say, "inner guidance."

If so, stop, and ask, "What's that about?"

Could there be some "doubt" still lingering?

What is your body, the barometer, communicating with you?

Are you feeling that following your inner guidance means that you have no control because you aren't using your common sense? Could you be feeling, "I'll lose control"?

Notice the thoughts that you are receiving as you are asking what your body, the barometer, is communicating.

Are you feeling resistance about the whole process of truly living a life where you are Trusting Your Superpower?

If you are, it's great that you are noticing this now, because you have been carrying resistance with you all the time. It's like a backpack.

How would it feel to put resistance down?

Do you feel a difference in your body letting go of resistance?

If you have been walking or carrying resistance for most of your life, you may feel like you are letting go of a very dear friend.

Ask yourself, does resistance, like that friend, still have a benefit in your life? Is it time to let resistance go?

Keep repeating the phrase out loud, slowly and consciously, "I Trust my Inner Guidance. I Trust my Inner Guidance. I Trust my Inner Guidance." Look in the mirror and connect with yourself and say "I Trust my Inner Guidance."

Are you starting to feel calmer and more confident as you are saying it?

Is there still stuff to clear?

There may be a slight sensation near your heart. It could be a little sensation, like a stretching of that space where your heart is, or energy is expanding your heart chakra. Consider that the stretching is the opening of your inner guidance connection more. An ever greater expansion is going on within you because you are opening to the greater more expansive Universe. "What you don't know, that you don't know."

You are constantly upgrading your software. There's more apps, more websites and more technology all the time. Everything around you is expanding, and consider that your heart and inner guidance must be recharged and upgraded too.

Keep updating. You can do the 10 day program a couple times a year, or more often. Notice how much more in tune you are becoming. Notice that you are enjoying the journey of your heart's desires.

The only constant thing is change, and how your inner guidance leads you will change because it is never consistent. It keeps up to date with everything in the Universe. It knows who is where, what is happening when, and what's best for you at all times. It is present, and in real time.

Remember how I was guided to book a flight to return home, 8 days before the virus was even named by the World Health Organization (WHO). I was safely back in my home country 9 days before WHO announced the global pandemic. I see and experience life completely differently to most people. Butterflies live in a different world than Caterpillars. Our world is full of Joy, Health, Peace, Love and Wealth, and we trust our Superpower to lead the way! Unique and perfect for each one of us!

You may feel like you are just beginning on this journey. It's perfectly okay. We all start somewhere. The principles are the same, whether you are starting or you feel you are close to having your wings being strong enough to surrender.

Keep doing the inner guidance Tune-In daily. This truly is the key. Do it whenever you feel like you are needing to be charged during the day. I usually Tune-In twice a day for a few minutes or until the stream ends. I trust that I'm always being given what I need, and I'm open to receive Joy, Health, Peace, Love and Wealth continually.

Treat your inner guidance, like you do your phone, your laptop, and make sure it is charged. I skipped saying treat it like you eat or sleep, because many of you have better charging habits for your technology than your body. Lol!

I encourage you to write in your notebook or Notes or share in the Facebook group when you have an inner guidance experience that surprises you or that you know will help others. The more you surround yourself with others who are trusting their inner guidance, the easier it is to follow your own inner guidance.

The conversations are different with people that trust their inner guidance.

Common phrases that you will hear are:

Trust the process.

Relax and stay in Joy.

Everything is happening for your highest and best good.

Let go and Surrender to the flow.

Everything you ever need is already inside you.

LIFE is for you to experience your heart's desires.

Your inner guidance always wants what's highest and best for you.

Your Superpower is so loud, it is easy for you to follow it.

Notice what you feel in your body as you read these phrases out loud?

I trust my intuition.

I am fully supported by the Universe.

My every need is always met.

Everything is in perfect order.

My inner guidance always leads me to my highest and best good.

I TRUST MY INNER GUIDANCE

If you just read the Tune-In at the beginning of this chapter, and still haven't tuned in yet…do it now.

Tune-In: Palms up, Body open, Happy thought

I'm asking for my inner guidance

To clearly communicate with me,

In each and every moment,

For my highest and best good.

I'm asking to be open to receive

This clear communication,

In each and every moment,

For my highest and best good.

And take joyful action on it.

Thank you!

Stay with the feeling in your body for as long as you can. Notice what you are experiencing. Are your palms warm? Are you feeling cold? Do you have tingles? Are you feeling at peace? Do you feel pain anywhere? If so, speak it out. Release it. When you're done receiving, take your hands to your heart, as if you are closing the drawbridge to your castle. You are fully charged, protected, and ready for your day.

Tune-In with ME

https://youtu.be/LNazErJFVgs

Step 3: Watch and/or Listen to Awaken an Aha in You

<u>Kate from England</u>

<u>Brenda from Ireland</u>

Again, congratulations on finishing Trusting Your Intuition - Discover Your Superpower in 10 Days. You are going to touch, move and inspire others to trust their inner guidance, and develop their Superpower as they notice how your life unfolds.

Buy them a book and seed into their life. Let them know they can subscribe to my YouTube channel and follow me on social media. You can refer them to me for a Heart Reset breakthrough session or join the waitlist together for the next group mentoring program through the Chrysalis of Transformation.

The whole planet is transforming, Healing from the Inside Out. By accepting the latest software update or downloading the newest app from me, you will be supported through your experiences as you journey to your Best Whole New World. It's all here, Joy, Health, Peace, Love and Wealth. Take advantage of my experiences and save yourself time and money by developing your Superpower!

I feel that is why I've had the journey I've had...to lead the way. The Butterfly world of Surrender - the Ultimate Trust exists. I'm here to shine the light back so you can find it. The new world isn't America, it's your Best Whole New World. The GPS to get there is inside you, and it's your Superpower. Your intuition/inner guidance is ready to get you there. Are you committed to getting there?

Open and receive your Best Whole New World, and all your heart's desires NOW!

GRATITUDE

The beautiful, talented and confident women, Faith and Destiny, who have blessed my life in infinite ways.

These gorgeous, authentic women who have shared their insights as they Learned to Trust their Inner Guidance in 10 days: Tina, Gale, Mena, Maria, Kate, Carolyne, Neltah, Brenda, Tulisa, Kat, Deb, Annelle, Christine, Hope, Sujata, Barbara, Shelly, Razia, Carol, Ragna, Shweta, and Elena.

Greta Hausler, whose mission was to keep the teachings of Bruno Groening alive and spread them around the world.

My spiritual family Sylke, Karin and Harlan

Rich who encouraged me to write a book.

To Flora for her commitment to her Health Transformation

My beautiful friend, Diana, who I guided through the chrysalis of transformation, and now has an amazing Superpower!

To all the men that have given me more clarity in trusting my inner guidance.

My dear friend, Carol, with her love and light, who was committed to every page of this book being representative of what comes through me.

Immense joy and gratitude for creating this with you!

Braco who gives silently in his gaze to all who are willing to receive.

Thank you for 25 years of service.

To all of those others who have been a spark in the light that has embraced me on this journey...thank you!

To all of you who have read this book, and are embracing your Superpower, look out world here we come....butterflies everywhere!

www.ingramcontent.com/pod-product-compliance
Lightning Source LLC
Chambersburg PA
CBHW022010090426
42741CB00007B/972